UNIVERSITY OF FLORIDA LIBRARIES

COLLEGE LIBRARY

PEACE or PESTILENCE

PEACE or PESTILENCE

BIOLOGICAL WARFARE AND HOW TO AVOID IT

by Theodor Rosebury

WHITTLESEY HOUSE
McGraw-Hill Book Company, Inc. New York · Toronto · London

CONTENTS

1.	Today's Questions	1
2.	How Much Can Be Told?	11
3.	Bacteriology for Beginners	18
4.	Bacteriology Upside Down	36
5.	The Scope of BW	50
6.	What Is a BW Agent?	62
7.	Potency	77
8.	Production	88
9.	Offense	98
10.	Defense	117
11.	International Control	136
12.	The Larger Problem	153
13.	Good, Bad, and Worse	169
14.	On the Positive Side	184
	Sources	199
	Index	211

The prolonged debate on the control of atomic energy and the demonstrations of the tremendously destructive power of atomic weapons that the United States has given to the world have distracted attention from developments in the field of bacteriological and lethal-chemical weapons. Whatever the situation regarding atomic weapons may have been or still may be, there has never been any effective monopoly of bacteriological and chemical weapons. Some of these weapons are probably potentially as destructive of human life as atomic weapons but not a single proposal has been made by any of the Member nations for any system of preventing or controlling their manufacture, nor has there been any discussion or study of the problem in the United Nations. Meanwhile, it is not too much to assume that, as in the case of atomic bombs, stocks of these weapons are piling up and that new discoveries are constantly being made that render them more deadly.

Nevertheless, all Members of the United Nations, including the great Powers, remain bound by their solemn pledge, made at the first session of the General Assembly almost two years ago, to eliminate all weapons of mass destruction and to reduce and regulate other armaments and, as an essential step to this end, to establish effective systems of international control, which will provide practical and effective safeguards, by way of inspection and other means, against the hazards of violations and evasions.

—From the Introduction by Trygvie Lie, dated July 5, 1948, to the United Nations Annual Report of the Secretary-General on the Work of the Organization, July 1, 1947–June 30, 1948. General Assembly Official Records: Third Session, Supplement No. 1 (A/565).

1. TODAY'S QUESTIONS

A FEW short years ago we came out of an adventure that cost us more than 20 million lives, more than a trillion dollars, and an additional price in destruction of property and in human misery that is beyond counting and will be a long, long time in the paying. Along with the bills we are now meeting for this war are demands for advance payments on another, which threatens to be incalculably more expensive. Here and abroad military men, who take seriously their assigned job of preparing for war and waging it, draw up the bills, approve them, and submit them for payment with the straight faces of men who know themselves as realists in a real world.

We dig down to pay and complain about high taxes. We are tired of war and have troubles of our own. This place where we live isn't what it ought to be; but after all, in these times one puts up with things. Yet this butcher's bill is really outrageous! The front pages of today's paper are depressing, but the sport pages are good clean fun, and the comic strips —*they* really ought to be on the front pages. The country seems to be overrun with spies; do you suppose that—but come and look at our new television set. Isn't it wonderful? Let's see what's on it now.

A baseball game, which almost immediately gives way to a solemn announcer, who speaks: *We interrupt this program with an important news bulletin. The President has just signed* an executive order giving Surgeon General Blank of the United States Public Health Service special powers to mobilize all necessary resources to combat the epidemic that started last Wednesday in St. Louis. Dr. Blank has asked us to make this announcement. There have been more than 4,000 deaths in St. Louis in five days, with a peak of 2,439 yesterday; but all indications are that the death toll will mount higher during the next few days. Cases of what are thought to be the same disease have been reported over an area of the Middle West from Chicago and Milwaukee to Memphis and from Kansas City to Indianapolis. Indianapolis reported 476 deaths yesterday. Local health authorities are working day and night with the aid of experts from Washington to determine the nature of the malady.

The source of the disease has not yet been discovered. The allegation made yesterday on the floor of the House by Representative Dash that this is a germ warfare attack of Russian origin has not been substantiated but is being thoroughly investigated. If it proves true we are assured by the Army High Command that extreme retaliatory measures will be taken at once with atomic as well as biological weapons.

In the meantime all possible steps are being taken to meet the emergency. Travel into and out of the affected area is being restricted, and quarantines are being imposed locally. You will be advised of regulations affecting your area by your press and radio. Meanwhile all citizens are urged to keep calm. Do not telephone local police or health departments. Cancel all unnecessary travel and stay at home if possible.

We return you now to Shibe Park.

It might start that way or in any of hundreds of other ways. Once it starts we will be in it up to our necks, with little if any choice but to go on with the dreary business to the bitter end. We will have little doubt that the end will be bitter, that neither we nor the enemy will have any hope of real victory. The power of destruction is now so great on both sides that, once let loose in the inexorable chain reaction of war, the clock of civilization may be turned back centuries, if not millennia. Perhaps we shall leave the world to the rats and the cockroaches, those unspecialized creatures who, the biologists sometimes tell us, have greater powers of survival than we. Or, if man is lucky, the more backward peoples of Africa and southern Asia may inherit the task of building a new world. Since they have fewer goods to covet than the inhabitants of more civilized parts of the globe they may escape the hottest flames of war. I can find some small comfort in the thought that, if they have the job to do, they can hardly make a worse mess of it than we have done.

We live in a critical time of great promise or dire threat. We have explored and colonized the last frontier and made the world small with airplanes and radio. Science has brought us to a point at which we might look forward with confidence to the conquest of disease and even to a true understanding of the life that animates us. And now we have cracked the atom and released such energies as hitherto only the sun and the stars could generate. But we have used the atom's energies to kill, and now we are fashioning weapons out of our knowledge of disease. Greed and a thoughtless faith in the inexhaustible bounty of the earth have led us to exploit the soil that feeds us until dust bowls have become deserts, and increasing areas of the globe, impoverished by neglect or devastated by war, can no longer support their inhabitants. Once when this happened, here or there, there was a land of promise across the sea or beyond the mountains; but now there is no place to go that man has not already fouled with his weapons and his avarice.

The seers tell us that we of our generation have a choice of alternatives and that we haven't much time to make it. We can choose to save our world for ourselves and our children, with science as our servant, helping us to restore and to build, finding new sources of power for us and new ways to use the old sources. There is still hope that all this can be done, although only if we do it soon. Or we can choose the easier road, the road of hate and fear that would lead us to destroy our neighbors because we don't like the way they live and because we are sure they are threatening to destroy us.

I am not a pessimist, but it seems to me that there is only one tenable basis for optimism in today's world, and that is a mature understanding of the issues we face, an understanding widely disseminated among the peoples of the world who pay the bills for war. I believe that sound understanding will direct a sound choice.

If you read what I write you have doubtless read what others have written on atomic energy and have a good idea of its capacity both for destruction and for constructive ends. You have seen germ warfare linked with atomic warfare in the newspapers, but you are not likely to know very much about germs as weapons, because not much authentic information on the subject has been made easily accessible to the general public. We have the technically detailed Smyth Report on *Atomic Energy for Military Purposes*—the fountainhead of a large literature on the atomic bomb—and we have read descriptions and seen vivid pictures of the explosions at Hiroshima, Nagasaki, and Bikini. But all we have on germ warfare is a few rather niggardly official handouts, some obscure technical reports, and a scattering of newspaper and magazine stories in which solid substance is hard to find under the froth of conflicting opinion and speculation. We are told on the one hand that germ warfare is even worse than atomic warfare and on the other that it won't be used because it would backfire too badly on anyone who tried it. Even bacteriologists know little about it unless they have been especially informed or have taken considerable pains to look into the subject; and among the general public all over the world there is a vast and very dangerous ignorance of it.

If we are heading into World War III we had better find out what we are letting ourselves in for. If it is going to be a bacteriological as well as an atomic war, what will it be like? We may be reasonably safe for a while on the atomic side, for we are told that it will be many years before any other nation can hope to catch up with us in making atomic bombs. But is this also true of germ warfare? Or may other nations have as much experience as we right now, if not more? We need answers to these questions, and we will be wise not to accept anybody's ready-made answers to them but to get at the facts so that we can find our own answers. It is my aim in this book to give you the facts.

My interest in germ warfare goes back to the years of Hitler's rise to power, when an occasional newspaper feature article dealing with the then seemingly remote prospect of war mentioned the possible use of germs as weapons. I have neither saved these stories nor bothered to search them out, but I remember them as diverting a small trickle off the current of thought I was then devoting, as a teacher of bacteriology, to the study of epidemic disease. The trickle continued as not much more while the clouds of war mounted over China, Ethiopia, and Europe; at most this was a subject for light conversation with colleagues at luncheon.

But even so small a trickle of thought seemed to be rare among bacteriologists right up to and beyond Pearl Harbor. Early in 1942 I could find no indication that any serious consideration was being given in this country to the possibility that the enemy might use germ warfare against us and to what was beginning to emerge in my mind as the consequently serious need for us to do something about it. We have since learned from Mr. George W. Merck, who wrote the official U.S. Army release, that this danger had been considered as early as the fall of 1941, when the matter was brought secretly to the attention of the War Department, and that the United States biological-warfare project had its origin at this time; but like other private citizens I knew nothing of all this. Consequently I sought and obtained authorization to prepare a detailed technical analysis of the subject of germ warfare,* and proceeded to do so with the aid of two colleagues, Dr. Elvin A. Kabat, a biochemist, and Martin H. Boldt, at that time a medical student. Our ninety-page report was completed and submitted to the National Research Council on June 8, 1942. We called it "Bacterial Warfare; a Critical Analysis of the Available Agents, Their Possible Military Applications, and the Means for Protection against Them." It was then and has remained an unofficial document, based only on open sources—a kind of report that might have been written anywhere in the world by persons capable of assimilating the technical literature. We undertook voluntarily to keep it secret during the war but had it published after the removal of wartime restrictions. It appeared in May, 1947, in the *Journal of Immunology*. At present it is out of print and obtainable only in technical libraries.

All three of us later became associated actively with the government's biological-warfare project. This project began with the appointment by the National Academy of Sciences, at the request of Secretary Stimson, of a group known as the WBC Committee, which surveyed the problem and presented its report in February, 1942. Except for a single paragraph, which Mr. Merck revealed in an address in May, 1946, this report has remained secret. The paragraph reads:

"The value of biological warfare will be a debatable question until it has been clearly proven or disproven by experi-

---

* I was stimulated to do this after several discussions of the possibilities of biological warfare with a small group of fellow members of the American Association of Scientific Workers, which was then actively concerned with promoting the fuller utilization of scientists in the war effort.

ence. The wise assumption is that any method which appears to offer advantages to a nation at war will be vigorously employed by that nation. There is but one logical course to pursue—namely, to study the possibilities of such warfare from every angle, make every preparation for reducing its effectiveness, and thereby reduce the likelihood of its use."

Following the recommendations in this report a civilian agency with the unrevealing name of War Research Service (WRS) was organized in the summer of 1942 under the Federal Security Agency, with Mr. Merck as director. For a time this agency operated only through existing government and private institutions, including the Army, Navy, and Public Health Service. It had as advisers a group of prominent scientists known cryptically as the ABC Committee, later as the DEF Committee. As the program developed, at first slowly, it became apparent that more extensive facilities were needed for it; and in November, 1942, WRS requested the Army's Chemical Warfare Service (CWS) to prepare to take over a larger scale research-and-development program. Construction of a principal installation was begun in April, 1943, at Camp Detrick, near Frederick, Maryland. Camp Detrick was operated by CWS under the general supervision of WRS until June, 1944, when by direction of President Roosevelt CWS assumed full responsibility for the program with the continuing cooperation of the Navy and the Public Health Service. At this point Mr. Merck became Special Consultant for Biological Warfare to the Secretary of War and chairman of the United States Biological Warfare Committee, which served to advise the Secretary of War on policy matters and to maintain liaison with British and Canadian biological-warfare groups.

In addition to Camp Detrick, the parent research and pilot-plant center for biological warfare, field-testing facilities were later established in Mississippi and in Utah, and a plant designed for the investigation of larger scale production was set up in Indiana.

At peak the biological-warfare project, still known guardedly as the Special Projects Division of CWS, had a total personnel of nearly 3,900, of which some 2,800 were Army personnel, nearly 1,000 Navy, and nearly 100 civilian, all "working together in the closest cooperation. They worked under high pressure and the strictest secrecy. Their achievements have been most remarkable." These are Mr. Merck's words. The work proceeded under the goad of intelligence reports which indicated that both the Germans and the Japanese were also developing biological warfare, reports that were confirmed by the war's end. But, again quoting Mr. Merck, in January, 1946, "all evidence to date indicates that the Axis powers were behind the United States, the United Kingdom, and Canada in their work on biological warfare."

Mr. Merck closes his report with these observations:

"While it is true that biological warfare is still in the realm of theory rather than fact, in the sense that it has not actually been used in military operations, the findings of the United States in this field along with the findings of groups engaged in similar work in the United Kingdom and Canada have shown that this type of warfare cannot be discounted by those of this nation who are concerned with the national security. Our endeavors during the war provided means of defending the nation against biological warfare in terms of its presently known potentialities and explored means of retaliation which might have been used had such a course been necessary. Although remarkable achievements can be recorded, the metes and bounds of this type of warfare have by no means been completely measured. Work in this field, born of the necessity of war, cannot be ignored in time of peace; and it must be continued on a sufficient scale to provide an adequate defense."

There follows a short paragraph which I shall cite later, and then this concluding statement:

✗ "In whatever deliberations that take place concerning the implementation of a lasting peace in the world, the potentialities of biological warfare cannot safely be ignored."

Amen.

As international tension mounted after the end of the war the Army, having lifted ever so slightly the lid of the germ-warfare Pandora's box, slammed it shut again under strict secrecy regulations. But it is no secret that work at Camp Detrick continues. Soon after the Merck Report appeared, for instance, Colonel Henry M. Black, commanding officer of Camp Detrick, stated that the camp would become a permanent Army installation and, as a newspaper story put it, "will continue the research that was done in the strictest of wartime secrecy, when steps were taken to combat biological-warfare developments that enemy governments might design for use against the United States." And Hanson W. Baldwin, writer on military affairs for *The New York Times*, reported several months later that "experimentation and production of some lethal toxins are continuing under the general supervision of the Chemical Warfare Service of the Army." many technical reports have been issued from Camp Detrick, among which the most recent, which may represent postwar research, reveal no immediate connection with biological warfare. It may be assumed that fundamental as well as practical research is necessary for the development of this subject, and it is possible that only papers dealing with the former sort of work are now being released for publication.

I found the following interesting note in the middle of an AP story that appeared in the spring of 1948 under the headline ARMY "SECRETS" GET AIRING IN CONGRESS TALKS:

"A little item relating to bacterial warfare, a secret that currently rates with the atom bomb, lists a $862,830 appropriation for 'Camp Detrick, Maryland.' (Before the military clamped the new supersecret classification on the whole subject of germ-warfare development it had announced that experimentations were being carried on at Camp Detrick.)"

We must respect military secrecy, but at the same time we must also find whatever means we can to participate as enlightened citizens of a democracy in the "deliberations . . . concerning the implementation of a lasting peace in the world." A lasting peace is our very direct concern; it is much too important a matter to each of us to be left complacently in the hands of others, however wise and trustworthy they may be. And since in these deliberations "the potentialities of biological warfare cannot safely be ignored," we must do the best we can to inform ourselves about biological warfare, with all respect for military secrecy but without letting it paralyze us. We can manage.

2. HOW MUCH CAN BE TOLD?

THE subject of biological warfare ("BW") has been covered by command of the armed forces of the United States with "a mantle of secrecy surpassing that surrounding the atomic bomb," according to an AP wire story in the *New York Herald Tribune* on December 1, 1947. Similar statements had appeared in the newspapers earlier, in January and again in September of the same year. After the first story appeared, the *San Francisco Chronicle*, having remarked in an editorial that "the lay public, as well as the scientists, is colossally underinformed" on the subject, went on to make this cogent suggestion:

"To understand germ warfare, as fully as it understands, for instance, atomic warfare, the public would have to know what it is, how dangerous it is, what bacteria would be used, what countermeasures could be taken, and how effective they would be. Yet to disclose these matters fully would rupture the security that exists, for they are just what a potential adversary of the United States would like to know.

"The Army would do well to consider the possibility of striking a compromise that would serve its own interests and the public's too. That would be to publish a well-organized, official report on germ warfare, comparable to the Smyth Report on *Atomic Energy for Military Purposes*. It should serve to clear the air as much as national security will permit the air to be cleared."

No such official report has appeared, and the temper of the times suggests that none is likely to appear. The military, in fact, is in an awkward position here. It could hardly hope to put out an official report that would satisfy the *San Francisco Chronicle* and at the same time preserve secrecy. "Compromise" between these two objectives would be extremely difficult, and it is not hard to understand why the Army might therefore have preferred to maintain its "no-talk" policy. Hence the difficulty for the American public remains. That our government is neither blind to this difficulty nor unsympathetic about it is indicated by the official view of the United States State Department on atomic energy, given as one of a group of "provisional conclusions" in a public document released in June, 1948. This conclusion is:

"That the people of the United States as a whole—and not merely those with a special or professional interest in the subject—must concern themselves with acquiring an adequate understanding of the essential facts about atomic energy and of the proposed international control measures on which their future security may depend. The same obligation falls upon the peoples of other nations."

But if our government is not in a position to help us much in doing our duty toward BW, it is not impossible for us to do an adequate job without its help and without in any way jeopardizing military secrecy. There is a considerable amount of freely published information which either deals plainly with BW or can be made to deal with it by putting two and two together. Anyone capable of understanding the technical literature of bacteriology and related sciences could compile this information into an adequate treatise on BW. There are persons competent to do such a job in every civilized country on earth. The information is as freely available to them as it is to us, and if they needed a stimulus to do it they may have received one in the next-to-the-last paragraph of the official Merck Report on BW, which reads:

"It is important to note that, unlike the development of the atomic bomb and other secret weapons during the war, the development of agents for biological warfare is possible in many countries, large and small, without vast expenditures of money or the construction of huge production facilities. It is clear that the development of biological warfare could very well proceed in many countries, perhaps under the guise of legitimate medical or bacteriological research."

I think the American public ought to have as much information as is freely available to every foreign government, particularly since most of it comes from American sources.*

Let me make one point perfectly clear: there are no military secrets in this book. Every statement of fact that I make is taken from unrestricted published sources. Every statement of opinion, moreover, is either credited to its source, official or otherwise, or else is my own. Those opinions that I offer as my own are based either on the facts or on background information and principles in the field of bacteriology which are universal knowledge throughout the world. And I shall include enough of these general principles to enable you to follow what I say even though you have no prior technical knowledge of the subject.

For the sake of the reader with a specialized interest in BW there are specific reference citations in an appendix at the end. The general reader, for whom this book is principally

---

* Although the Merck Report speaks of British and Canadian BW activities, I have seen only one report giving details—on an extensive joint United States–Canadian research project dealing with a disease of cattle called "rinderpest." Mr. Merck also alludes to German and Japanese experiments on BW, and there are other scattered references to these two countries and to possible developments in the Soviet Union. These are mentioned in appropriate places in succeeding pages. On BW in other countries I have seen no published information at all.

intended, is likely to find the going easier if he is not continually tripped up by references interpolated in the text. But both groups, who may share a common belief that there is very little information on BW available to the general public, may wish to know at this point what my principal sources have been.

There are five groups of sources of BW information. One may be called "historical." It comprises articles on BW published in many parts of the world before World War II. Most of the twenty-odd articles of this kind that I have seen appeared in medical or other technical journals. But since modern BW is very largely a product of World War II this early material has the somewhat stale flavor of ancient history. I have drawn upon it sparingly and used it only where it seemed to further our principal aim of understanding BW as a present-day phenomenon.

In a second category are four sources that may be called "official and nontechnical." The first is the War Department press release on BW of January 3, 1946, prepared by Mr. George W. Merck, Special Consultant for Biological Warfare; I shall speak of this hereafter as the "Merck Report." The second is the United States Navy release dealing with a separate BW project at the University of California, which appeared in the newspapers on the day after the Merck Report. The third is Mr. Merck's address in May, 1946, to the Westinghouse Forum, on "Peacetime Implications of Biological Warfare," which may be accepted as official. And the fourth, prepared by Mr. Merck with the aid of three other scientists, is included in "Scientific Information Transmitted to the United Nations Atomic Energy Commission" in 1946 by the Department of State. The Navy statement is the shortest of the four, but all of them are brief. They give the impression that they say less than they leave unsaid, and several include some identical passages. They are, however, the most important of our sources because of their official nature.

In the next group of unofficial technical sources one is so much more important to us than any others that I shall mention it alone. This is the Rosebury-Kabat-Boldt Report, originally prepared in 1942 but not made public until 1947. It is the most extensive statement of the principles of BW in the published literature. Since it was put out in its original form, which depended only on open sources available before the United States BW project was started, it necessarily omits wartime developments and makes no mention of any changes in principles that may have been made in the course of wartime experience. Yet it serves sufficiently well as a framework for this book, a scaffolding upon which it is possible to arrange material from all our sources into a coherent structure. I shall speak of it hereafter as the "1942 Report."

The unofficial nontechnical sources are many and varied both in kind and in their usefulness to us. There are magazine articles and newspaper stories, based on the official releases, on the 1942 Report, on official technical sources, and on a medley of rumors, presumed "leaks" and miscellaneous notions. Much of this is valuable material, but it is sometimes impossible for the uninitiated to distinguish between the grain and the chaff in it; nor can I do more here, unless I find substantiation or contradiction in one of the other sources or in established principles. This group of sources will therefore serve us in an interpretive capacity rather than as part of the basis of fact upon which to build our understanding of BW.

The final group of sources, the official technical ones, comprises approximately one hundred fifty papers in the scientific literature which with few exceptions—where BW is alluded to—can be identified with our subject only by their point of origin, which is given as Camp Detrick, Frederick, Maryland.

Since the official releases mentioned Camp Detrick as "the parent research and pilot-plant center" of the American BW development, any foreign agent interested in BW will have read these reports with a special kind of interest. Nobody need suppose that they present in aggregate a complete picture of the technical aspects of BW. They reveal, avowedly, only those contributions from wartime BW research that could "be published without endangering the national security," and, indeed, they were released under a liberal policy because of their "great value to public health, agriculture, industry, and the fundamental sciences." (These phrases are from the Merck Report.) They are nevertheless very useful to us in the construction of our mosaic of BW. Fitted into place within the framework, they fill some of the gaps in the official releases and supply several useful bits and details with which to round out the picture given in the 1942 report.

It is obvious that all of this does not add up to a complete account of biological warfare, but I should not have attempted to make this book complete even if it did. It is not my purpose to teach you how to kill people with germs, although you should know something about how this might be done, just as the prosecutor must understand the ways of murderers if he is to cope with them successfully. Our purpose is to understand BW in order to search for ways to control or eliminate it; and this does not require an exhaustive treatment of every phase of the subject.

But of the information available to us I shall omit nothing that seems relevant. As you will see, I have some fairly well-developed opinions regarding both the technical aspects and the political and moral implications of BW. Yet I propose to proceed in a manner that seems to me appropriate for a scientist who holds that democracy is the most effective principle of government thus far devised. I intend to give you the facts of BW as objectively as I can and to keep my conclusions within their bounds. Even the political problems toward which BW points can be approached in the same spirit. Moral problems will have to be handled less scientifically because they are in their nature less scientific. But wherever it seems advisable to offer my own opinions I shall label them as such. The facts you can, if you wish, verify from their sources. The opinions will either seem to flow from the facts and therefore be acceptable to you; or else you will find them unjustified by the facts and will reject them.

Having stated these high resolves, it seems necessary to admit that I cannot hope to be altogether successful in fulfilling them. This will be true for two reasons. One is that in some strategic places the facts will be insufficient to justify really scientific conclusions; and here it will be necessary to suggest tentative conclusions on a pragmatic basis—because, of several possible alternatives, these seem to lead to the most or perhaps to the only useful consequences. The second reason is that our subject matter necessarily extends in several directions beyond the boundaries to which science is thus far limited. It may be questioned whether a scientist, not being disembodied, can ever quite dissociate himself from feeling and approach any subject, however circumscribed, with quite complete objectivity. But with a subject that ramifies as BW does from its scientific stem into social, political, and ethical branches, it is certainly not possible for a writer, be he ever so scientific, to achieve perfect detachment. Nor does it seem to me to be desirable. Our over-all concern in this book is with a great human problem rather than with one that is scientific alone; and as I approach it I shall have to exercise the right of a scientist to be a human being.

3. BACTERIOLOGY FOR BEGINNERS

DESPITE Hiroshima, anyone who has not made a conscious effort to understand the meaning of nuclear physics will have no inkling of it; but the same fellow is sure to have some knowledge of bacteriology through personal experience. He has seen the edges of a cut on his finger redden and swell with pus; he remembers a bout with scarlet fever or diphtheria; he knows the look and smell of rotten meat, of cider turned to vinegar, of milk separated into curds and whey. He may have only the vaguest glimmering of an idea that bacteria play a part in all these processes; but he knows the processes themselves, and so he knows something of the science of bacteriology.

Yet I have seen this word "bacteriology" completely fail to ring a bell in the minds of otherwise well-informed men. About ten years ago at a social gathering a colleague and I were introduced as "bacteriologists" to two prosperous businessmen who found the word baffling. We undertook to explain that we dealt with bacteria—things that cause infection—microbes, germs, bugs. This seemed to satisfy one of them, but the other knitted his brows over the new idea for a while and then found a question for us: "You deal in germs, bugs—yes; but where do you find your customers?" As I remember we spent the rest of the evening talking politics.

Nearly everyone must know at least a little about nuclear

physics by now, or the legion of scientists and science writers who have been laboring to explain the atomic bomb to us since the Smyth Report appeared in 1945 have been wasting their time. If you do, you will have no trouble understanding enough of bacteriology to make a good citizen's use of the knowledge. My subject is intrinsically simpler—or so it seems to me!—and you don't need to know quite so much of it. Some elementary principles and the meaning of a few words should be enough to see you through this book, and this book should be enough to get you well started, at least, on the whole issue of BW. But first, the elementary principles and the words.

"Bacteriology" itself covers more than the dictionary says. Bacteria are not the only things we study; they are one among several groups of "things" for which there is no all-inclusive name. "Germs" comes about as close as we can get to an over-all term. From the human viewpoint there are good germs, bad ones, and indifferent ones. We care only about the bad ones, which we may call "agents of infection." An agent of infection is merely a "thing" that causes infection. It is usually a *living* thing, but some—the so-called "viruses"—are in a no-man's land between living and nonliving. Bacteriologists themselves have been trying to pull them over to one side or the other since 1935, when Wendell M. Stanley found that a virus which infects tobacco plants is a single pure substance.

All the agents of infection that we need be concerned with —and all those that come within the ken of the bacteriologist —have two properties in common and probably only two. They are so tiny that we can't see them individually * ex-

* Almost any attempt at precision in the definition of biological terms is likely to lead to trouble, and I must compromise between two conflicting needs—not to mislead the uninformed reader into oversimplification and not to insert so many qualifying phrases or words like "usually," "perhaps," or "roughly" as to leave my meaning unclear. In the text above, for example, I have inserted the word "individually" because we can see germs in the aggregate easily enough—as you have seen mold growing on bread, a cake of

cept with a very high-powered microscope or not even then; and they are all able to reproduce their kind inside the body of some larger living thing. In two words, they are minute parasites. Let's call them "germs."

There are seven or eight different broad classes, or kinds, of germs, with many different sorts in each class. Think of them as being arranged, not in a straight line, but like the trunk and branches of a tree.

The bacteria proper are the trunk. They are the trunk, indeed, not only of the tree of germs but probably of the whole tree of life; for it is very likely that certain kinds of bacteria were the very first living things on earth and that all other living things evolved from them. They are usually called "plants," but it seems more useful to think of them as neither plant nor animal but somewhere in between. Groups of branches grow out of the trunk in three directions.

On a branch leading to the animal kingdom are the *protozoa*, or microscopic animals, and nearer the trunk on the same branch or a nearby one, between the protozoa and the bacteria, are the *spirochetes*. On the other side, leading to the vegetable world, are the *fungi*, or molds and yeasts. And again intermediately placed are the *actinomycetes*, midway between fungi and bacteria. Off in a third direction, leading this time in defiance of analogy away from the tree of life, is a branch or cluster of branches bearing first a queer little group of germs called the *pleuropneumonia* forms, then the *rickettsiae*, and then, leading into or connecting with the nonliving chemical and physical world of molecules and atoms, the *viruses*.

Among the bacteria themselves there are plantlike forms

---

yeast, or bacteria swarming as a cloud in spoiled wine. Since the purpose of this book is a serious one I shall have to risk some loss of clarity in order not to do too much violence to precision; and I hope the discerning reader (or the carping critic) will be discerning enough to recognize that if it is hard to read parts of this book it was even harder to write them.

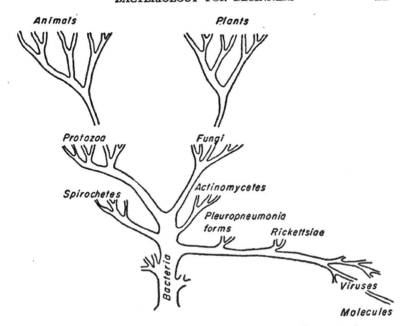

Fig. 1. *The tree of life, simplified and highly speculative. This diagram is intended to suggest relationships among different kinds of germs and between germs and animals, plants and the nonliving world. Evolution may have proceeded from the trunk to the branches, but nobody can be sure of this. Unnamed branches indicate that the bacteria themselves are varied.*

that can get nourishment, as green plants do, from very simple foods—carbon dioxide from the air, water and nitrogen from the soil, and everything else in the form of simple mineral salts. Other bacteria and many members of all the other groups of germs depend like animals directly on the rest of the living world for preformed living substance in a greater or lesser state of complexity. All the agents of infection fall into this second group; hence their predilection for growing inside of other living things, where they produce infection.

The unit of length used for measuring bacteria under the microscope is the micron, a metric unit equal to $\frac{1}{1000}$ of a millimeter or, roughly, $\frac{1}{25000}$ of an inch. Ball-shaped bacteria (*cocci*) are usually 1 micron in diameter or less. Stick or rod-shaped ones (*bacilli*) and curved or corkscrew-shaped ones (*vibrios* or *spirilla*) are both anywhere from $\frac{1}{5}$ micron to more than 1 micron thick and 2 to 10 or more microns

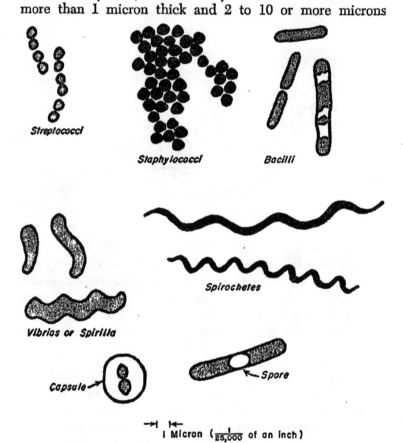

FIG. 2. *How bacteria look under the microscope.*

long. The protozoa are mostly much larger than the bacteria, often ten to twenty times as big—big enough to show, under the microscope, the nucleus and other parts characteristic of all living cells. The spirochetes are thin, flexible, corkscrew-shaped germs, mainly about $1/10$ micron thick but as much as 20 microns long. Like the bacteria and the disease-producing fungi they are too small to show a nucleus or many other details of their structure under the microscope. But by special methods applied in recent years it has become plain that bacteria have nuclei, and most bacteriologists think of them now as true living cells, although once we believed them to be something different.

Although they do not have easily visible nuclei many bacteria show a few structural details, two of which are of interest to us. One is a cloak or layer of material outside the bacterium and different from it in appearance. This so-called *capsule* is often typical of disease-producing germs as opposed to their weaker or less harmful relatives, which may appear naked. The other internal detail is found in only a few kinds of bacilli; it is a tiny glistening round or oval granule called a *spore*. This bacterial spore is very much harder to kill than the germ itself. It permits the germ to stay alive where a germ without a spore would be destroyed.

The fungi are again usually larger than the bacteria; but the three forms on the odd branch—the pleuropneumonia forms, the rickettsiae, and the viruses—range downward from the size of the smallest bacteria to about $1/100$ micron for the smallest viruses, which is no larger than some of the big protein molecules—and this, it seems, is what these viruses are.

Among these germs only the protozoa, the spirochetes, and the fungi are big enough to make their intensive study merely by observation through the microscope very rewarding. Just by looking at them on a slide it is usually possible for an expert to identify them as you identify a cat or an oak tree by looking at it. The bacteria, with a few exceptions, and the odd forms without exception are too small for this sort of thing. Nobody, however expert, can tell the difference between the relatively harmless colon bacillus and the germ of typhoid fever just by looking at them. All the rickettsiae—and there are many different kinds—look deceptively alike; while for the most part the microscope cannot even tell us that we are seeing a virus, much less which one of several score viruses it may be.

Partly for this reason but mainly because these germs are so important to us in our daily lives, we are much more interested in what they do than in what they look like; and it is by their deeds rather than their faces that we recognize them. The way they grow and the sort of food they need, the changes they bring about in the food as they grow, and the things that happen when they get inside larger living things—these properties of germs differ in many ways, both obvious and subtle; and it is their differences more than their appearances that let us tell them apart. The streptococcus that causes blood poisoning may look exactly like the one that grows in everybody's mouth and usually does no harm at all; but the first can dissolve the red cells of blood from a sheep or rabbit, while the second can't. A little fluid taken from a pock on a man with smallpox, when scratched into the skin of a monkey, causes a typical pock in the monkey. The closely related but slightly different cowpox virus has a similar effect in the skin of a rabbit. Coughings or garglings from a person in the early stage of influenza, if dropped into the nose of a ferret, can make it sick with a characteristic fever. It would be interesting to know just what these viruses look like, but we can recognize them well enough without seeing them.

The disease process—the infection itself—is at the center

of our interest in germs, whether we examine the process in order to identify the germ or the disease or study it to learn how the disease is caused or how to cure or control it. An infection is a sort of battle between you (or an animal or plant) and some kind of germ that has found its way into your body and has proceeded to set up housekeeping there and raise a large family. You win by destroying the agent or vice versa. You are the unwilling host. "Host" is the technical term for the larger living thing inside of which the germ —the "parasite"—attempts to be fruitful and multiply. Occasionally this is a mutually beneficial arrangement, as when certain special kinds of bacteria form nodules, or little tumors, on the roots of beans or peas. These root-nodule bacteria derive their nourishment from the plant, and in this sense they are parasites and the plant is their host; but in return the bacteria "fix" the nitrogen of the air by converting it into nitrates, a form required by the plant for its own nourishment. More often the host-parasite engagement is harmful —mutually harmful, in fact, although we need not waste our sympathy on the germs. If it is harmful enough so that the host is inconvenienced by it or is likely to be when the parasitic family gets big enough, we speak of the process as an "infection."

Like all other living things parasites are somehow urged to perpetuate their own kind. If they depend on parasitism for their livelihood they can't go on living for very long unless they have means worked out for getting into the right sort of host, reaching a place inside his body where they can be comfortable, and later assuring for their progeny some means of escape to the outside world or through it to a new host. The right kind of host is essential. A germ that parasitizes plants can rarely survive in an animal; one may like a horse but not a cow; another may find a lazy and relatively peaceful life in the rat but only strife and turbulence in man—the feeling, in this instance, being in all probability mutual. Some of the most serious of human diseases, as the great American bacteriologist Theobald Smith pointed out long ago, are due to accidents of a sort, in which a parasite gets into a host in whose body it can manage somewhat but not well, so that things rapidly go wrong for both. It is doubtless to the parasite's advantage to keep the host in a reasonably good humor so that he will stay around for a while and not fight too hard; if he dies most if not all the parasites must die with him.

But having found the right kind of host, the parasite must also get in through the right portal. The bacillus of typhoid fever or the vibrio of cholera can make no headway if introduced into or through the human skin; they prefer the mouth. The protozoan parasite of malaria must find its way directly into the blood, being jabbed home by an obliging mosquito. The coccus of lobar pneumonia ("pneumococcus") or the tubercle bacillus prefer the nose and throat, highroad to the lungs. Some germs, to be sure, are less particular on this score. The disease-producing streptococcus can manage well enough for itself under the skin, in the blood, or in the nose, throat, or lungs; while other bacteria that we shall speak of later (like the bacilli of brucellosis or of tularemia) can get in through the unbroken skin or by any of several other pathways.

Once it is inside the host the germ may be content to settle where it lands—in the skin, the throat, the lungs, or the blood—or it may have to find its way to a place that particularly appeals to it before starting to colonize. The typhoid bacillus likes the tonsils or adenoids or patches of the same kind of soil in the wall of the intestine. When a man is bitten by a dog infected with rabies, or hydrophobia, the virus of this disease must find a nerve and travel along it to the brain to reach soil suitable for its development.

And from its place of residence in one host the agent—or more likely its progeny many generations removed—must get out to attack a new host or else risk extermination when death turns off the heat. If the agent is on the skin or on the surface of a natural body opening, simple contact with a new host may transfer it, as happens with the spirochete of syphilis or the coccus of gonorrhea ("gonococcus"). Or, if the agent can stay alive for a long enough time between hosts in the cold world, it may complete its host-to-host cycle by delayed or indirect contact, as the fungus of athlete's foot does when it waits on the floor of a locker room for a naked foot. Agents that have made their home in the lungs, and in so doing have given rise to local irritation, provoke a cough that expels them into the air for others to breathe or at least raises them into the nose and mouth, from which a sneeze does a more effective job of spraying them outward. The resulting atomized droplets may pass directly to a new host if he happens to be standing in the path of the cough or sneeze. More commonly they settle and dry but stay alive long enough to be raised with dust by air currents or movements and so find their way later into a new host's breathing passage; or they dry without settling, remain suspended in the air, and so accomplish a similar transit. If they are colonizing in the bowel or are able to reach it from their place of residence somewhere else—as the typhoid bacillus does by growing in the gall bladder and passing outward via the bile duct—the germs reach the outside world in the stool, from which, directly or with the aid of flies or unwashed hands, they may find their way through drinking water or food to the mouths of new hosts. And, finally, if the agent has no way of reaching the outside world unaided but is present in the circulating blood, an obliging insect, drinking from the skin capillaries, may pick it up, nourish it within its own body for a while, and then give it back through the well it drills in a new host. Thus with the rickettsia of typhus fever, the virus of yellow fever, the protozoan of malaria, and many other agents. In this kind of transit, with few exceptions, the transmitting insect or other bloodsucker (it may be an eight-legged creature like a tick or mite) must be of just the right sort for the agent. For typhus it is the human body louse, for yellow fever the *Aëdes aegypti* mosquito, for malaria a mosquito of the genus *Anopheles*. Such insects or ticks we call "*vectors* of infection."

It will be plain that by any of these means of transit the agent may pass from one host not just to a single new one but to many. The direct-contact road and transmission through vectors require that each new infection be a separate event; but there may nevertheless be many such. A prostitute with syphilis or gonorrhea or the virus disease called *lymphogranuloma venereum* may infect men by the score, and each of these may pass the agent on to many women. More than one *Aëdes* mosquito may bite a single yellow-fever patient, and each mosquito may in turn bite more than one new victim. The other routes of transmission—indirect contact, air transit, and the contamination of food or water—allow for simultaneous multiple new contacts. Any of these events may provoke spreading processes of infection through a population—"epidemics." The odds seem to be on the side of the agent here, and it may appear that the agent would soon overreach itself by destroying all its potential hosts; but there are compensating factors we have not yet looked at.

Not all agents have their host-to-host cycle quite perfected, or they may have it worked out well for one kind of host but not for another. Some of the germs that we shall need to talk about in relation to BW fall in this group, like the bacillus of brucellosis, which stays alive in cattle, goats, or swine, but generally reaches a dead end in the individual man because it finds no effective way of reaching a new human host. Even bubonic plague, as we shall see, although frightfully epidemic in man, stays alive through years or centuries in the bodies of rats and other wild rodents, infects man only by complicated accident, and cannot keep going indefinitely by transfer from man to man.

It may be helpful to draw a few fine distinctions. All infections are *transmissible*—meaning that all agents of infection, if they can find their way from one host to another, can continue indefinitely to generate infection. If they find the pathway of transmission blocked in nature, the scientist can help them by removing some of the agent from one host and deliberately injecting it with a syringe into another. Transmissibility is a potential attribute of all agents of infection; but it may imply artificial aid. Agents that can pass freely from host to host without artifice are *communicable,* and the infections they cause are the *communicable diseases.* This is the accepted term, although the word *contagious*—strictly a capacity for natural transmission of infection by *contact*—is often loosely used as a synonym. But the similar word *infectious* we had better avoid entirely, because it cannot fail to be ambiguous. Usage has colored it with the idea of communicability, as when we speak of "infectious laughter"; we need an adjective that implies nothing but a capacity for causing infection (necessarily transmissible, but not necessarily communicable), and for this the word *infective* suits our purpose well. We shall speak of "infective agents" as equivalent to "agents of infection."

Having followed the parasite through the process of infection in individuals and in crowds, we must now look at the other side in the battle—the host. Throughout this process the host does not remain passive; he fights back. The kind of fight he puts up largely determines the picture of infection as a whole. It helps the doctor recognize what is wrong with him; it spells the difference between recovery and death;

it helps to check epidemics; and incidentally it provides us with a battery of tools and means that we can use both to identify infective agents and to combat them.

If a staphylococcus capable of causing a boil gets into the skin of the back of a man's neck from a barber's razor—or when any infective agent reaches the point in its host where it can settle and multiply—nothing happens immediately. The scratch, of course, may bleed, and bleeding may cast off the germ so that nothing else happens at all. But the agent, having gained a foothold satisfactory for it, may have been torpid from lying idle for a while and may need an interval —minutes, hours, even days, or longer—before it can wake up and get busy. Likewise the defending cells of the host need time to be alerted to the presence of a foreign invader. If they can start their offensive before the agent gets going and wage it successfully, they may kill the germ and stop the process short. What happens will, in fact, depend mainly on the interplay of three forces—the infecting strength of each invading germ (its particular *virulence*, or *infectivity*, which we shall talk about later at length), the numbers of the invader, and the resistance of the host in terms of this particular kind of germ. But unless the invader is cast out before it can cause trouble there will be a lag before the host becomes grossly aware of its presence—the boil hurts, and he can feel it with his fingers; or he is uneasy and feverish; or he is suddenly violently sick. During this interval, the *incubation period* of the infection, the germs are multiplying and perhaps spreading from one part of the host to others, and the host is mobilizing his defenses and thereby, in greater or less degree, upsetting his normal economy much as a nation does in meeting the threat of war.

But now there is a boil, a cough, a fever, or a bellyache. Each of these and all the other symptoms that the sick man feels or the doctor sees is in some way a protective response of the fighting host. The local defenses have detected the growing staphylococcus. Neighboring blood vessels expand and make the skin red; they pour out germ-eating white blood cells which crowd around the cocci and try to swallow and destroy them; in so doing they disrupt the tissues and cause swelling and pain; and around them the local cells divide and lay down a barrier of new fibrous tissue. This is the process of acute inflammation. It hurts, but when successful it destroys the invading germs in a fluid mass of injured white blood cells—pus, which bores its way to the surface as the boil "points" and drains. It walls off the germs so that, if they are not quickly destroyed, they cannot penetrate the fibrous barrier and spread to other areas. The staphylococcus in the skin rarely causes more than a boil, because the local defenses against it are good, the inflammatory response is effective, and the abscess, having cast off the germs, heals and disappears, leaving a small scar of fibrous tissue. Unless the pus on its way out entered the skin of another host, that is the end of this particular family of staphylococci.

The same sort of thing may go on in the lung or the intestines, where the growing irritation of a local war may produce coughing or cramps, which may evict the invader completely and end the infection. But if the germ can jump this first hurdle, because it is itself powerful or because the defense is weak, the battle spreads out but is not over. With the local barriers down and the germs invading new territory, the host mobilizes his whole economy. He brings out reserve cells that may do a better job of germ eating than the little white cells of the blood. He steps up production of the white cells themselves; through internal exertion in the emergency of war his body temperature rises—he has fever. His energies are diverted to war so that he must cut down peaceful pursuits—he feels sick and must lie down. Even without outside aid the war may yet be won.

But by now the host is also doing something else. His tissues are reacting to the presence of the invader by producing new substances, or old substances changed so that they can be directed in special ways against this particular infective agent—the *antibodies* of the circulating blood. These are made especially for each germ and act on it alone—they are *specific*. If the germ gives out poisons—*toxins*—antibodies counteract them and make them nonpoisonous; these are *antitoxins*, a different one for each kind of poison. Or special antibodies may strip the protective cloak, or capsule, off such germs as the pneumococcus, which depends on its capsule to protect it against the host's germ-eating cells. Special antibodies can neutralize a virus or herd bacteria together into clumps so that the germ-eating cells can capture them in groups instead of having to hunt them down one by one. The antibodies are not the whole of the host's defense but only auxiliary weapons, more or less effective depending on the germ and the kind of battle it wages. Of the different kinds the antitoxins are the most useful, especially in those diseases in which the toxin is the germ's chief or only weapon—as in diphtheria and tetanus and in the peculiar kind of food poisoning called "botulism," which we shall learn more about later.

When the host recovers from infection he usually finds himself changed by the experience. He has his antibodies left, or he is left with a new ability to produce them quickly for the particular germ or toxin he has thrown off, if the need should arise again. In proportion as the antibodies were important to his recovery they give him immunity against another attack of the same disease. This immunity is a relative thing, never absolute for any disease, strongest against toxins and many of the viruses and rickettsiae, less effective against most bacteria that don't depend on toxins, and usually still less effective against the spirochetes, the fungi, the actinomycetes, and the protozoa.

But antibodies can be very potent defensive weapons, and we can take advantage of them to protect men and animals against infection in a way that by-passes the inconveniences and risks of illness. Antibodies are produced by the host in response to the presence of a foreign germ or of parts or products of a germ, like the capsule of the pneumococcus or the toxin of the diphtheria bacillus. If the germ itself or these aggressive parts or products can have their stings removed so that they can be deliberately but safely injected into the bodies of men or animals the antibodies will still be produced, and the host may be protected against the disease without having had much more than a little painful lump on his arm where the needle went in. Sometimes the germ may be killed, so that it can no longer infect but can nevertheless make the host produce useful antibodies against it. This is done with typhoid bacilli. Toxins can be made nonpoisonous with formalin without altering their ability to call forth antitoxins; such altered toxins are called *toxoids*. Or the germ may be altered without killing it, in a variety of ways, so that it either fails to infect the host that is to be protected or produces so mild or small an infection that inconvenience is minimized and recovery assured, making it a much better risk than the original disease. This is what is done to protect against smallpox; the virus of a closely related infection of cattle, cowpox, or *vaccinia,* can be gently pressed into the human skin with no more risk of serious injury than is involved in taking a bath or a railroad trip but with the accruing advantage of a very solid immunity against smallpox. You will recognize here the practice of *vaccination,* so called because vaccinia was the first infection thus deliberately given to man to protect him, by the Englishman, Edward Jenner, way back in

1796. Pasteur, nearly a century later, applied the practice to other infections but continued the use of the same name for them, so that any germ, dead or attenuated, or any germ part or product used to give this kind of protection is now called a *vaccine*, and the process of using it, vaccination.

Antibodies have another group of uses. Because they act specifically on particular kinds of germs or parts or products of germs and because their action can be seen or recognized in a variety of ways *outside* a host—in test tubes or under a microscope—they can be used to identify the germ or part or product or to help recognize the nature of an illness. Accordingly, if your doctor suspects that you may have typhoid fever, he sends a sample of your blood to a laboratory, where the clear serum prepared from it is mixed with a culture of typhoid bacilli and separately with cultures of related germs. If you do have the disease your blood will contain antibodies against the typhoid bacillus, and the laboratory technician will spot them by the presence of visible clumps of germs in this culture but not in the others. Or the scientist, having injected killed typhoid bacilli into the veins of a rabbit so as to make the animal produce antibodies, can use the rabbit's blood serum with the same test to identify a culture he suspects of being the typhoid bacillus. This study of antibodies and their laboratory uses as well as their uses in protection against infection has become a specialized subscience called *immunology*, of which we need only this brief introduction for the purposes of this book.

Knowing all these things about germs and hosts and the process of infection makes it possible for men to help the host in other ways. By studying each germ outside the host or in deliberately infected laboratory animals, they can search for new and better drugs to treat the infection. It is by this means that scientists within recent years have given us the sulfa drugs, penicillin, streptomycin, and other curative agents that by now have saved countless lives. And by learning more and more about the host-to-host cycle of each germ, the ways it selects to enter and infect the individual and to leave his body, its mode of transit through the environment and what makes it choose that mode, they can learn to apply controls so as to cut down or abolish the opportunities afforded to the germ for producing epidemics. We shall have more to say in later chapters about epidemics and the subscience that deals with them, *epidemiology*, properly the study of the behavior in populations, rather than in individuals, of any disease, infective or not. And we shall see that among the practices to which it has given rise—like the treatment of public water supplies to make them potable and other methods of public health—are to be found the most useful of all our weapons in the war against disease.

But now we come to another kind of war, war waged not against germs but with germs against men, animals, and plants—BW.

4. BACTERIOLOGY UPSIDE DOWN

IF you want to understand BW you must figuratively stand on your head. BW is an upside-down science, an inversion of nature. Normally we study disease in order to prevent it or cure it. This is bacteriology right side up. But BW sets out to produce disease. It is not normal or natural but abnormal and artificial. Yet it is curious and very significant that the abnormality and the artifice of BW don't just make it *different* from normal science; in important ways they make it easier, more predictable. In places where bacteriology right side up stalls or goes snailwise at the frontiers of knowledge, the topsy-turvy artificial science can find detours. This chapter tells why and in so doing explains a root principle of BW—the technical facility that artificiality gives it.

Natural bacteriology itself may seek to produce disease, but it does so only as a means to an end. The end is always control of disease by cure or prevention, based on understanding. Normally when we produce disease in laboratory animals our purpose is best served if the experimental process resembles the natural disease closely. But it is a curious fact that such duplication of natural disease is difficult. In the attempt to copy nature by experiment, artifice gets in the way. We can give dogs diabetes by removing their pancreas or by injecting into them a poison, alloxan, which injures part of the pancreas. But the result is not quite like diabetes in man, in which the pancreas is damaged by causes still unknown. Lobar pneumonia is caused by germs called pneumococci. When injected into mice these bacteria easily kill the animals, but the disease affects the whole body rather than just the lungs. Lung infections can be produced in animals with pneumococci, but not easily. And there are several important infections of man, including cholera, typhoid fever, cerebrospinal meningitis, and gonorrhea, for which there is no adequate experimental counterpart at all. The fact that we cannot reproduce these diseases experimentally impedes our progress toward their complete understanding. It is a block in the road to public health, but it need not bother BW. In war it would make little difference whether germs used as weapons reproduced natural diseases or reasonable facsimiles of them or something altogether different—so long as they were effective weapons.

BW does not have to be concerned with *natural* disease, and therefore it can find ways to go forward where natural science falters. Take plague, for instance. In nature this scourge of history develops only with the greatest difficulty; yet in the laboratory it can be reproduced with no trouble at all. Bubonic plague is spread in both animal and human populations almost exclusively by the rat flea. To produce plague in man, this degenerate * wingless parasite must be provided with a long chain of rather narrowly limited circumstances. It must first be on the back of a rat that has plague and feed on the rat's blood and plague bacilli. This rat must thereafter die, for the flea will not leave it to transport its cargo of bacilli elsewhere until the rat's body grows

---

* No moral judgment is intended. All animals are either parasitic like the flea or predatory like us. Most plants and some bacteria are nearly independent of other living things, but even these must have the products of decomposition of dead animals or plants. The flea is called "degenerate" because evolution toward its peculiar form of parasitism has cost it the wings of a complete insect. It is particularly unseemly for us to pass judgment on the flea so long as our behavior makes a book like this one possible.

cold. The flea must then acquire the right amount of infection. Plague bacilli must reproduce in its tiny forestomach up to the point where they crowd it and hamper the insect's free efforts to feed. Only the blocked flea is likely to transmit infection, when strenuous sucking tires it and the recoil of its germ-laden forestomach ejects bacilli into the flea bite. Reduced by near impotency to critical hunger, the flea must find itself a victim—another rat, or, failing rats, a man. It will usually not choose a man if it can find a rat; and large numbers of human beings are likely to be bitten by rat fleas only if most of the rats have already been killed off by plague. Since the wingless flea can't jump more than 5 inches, an obliging rat must bring it to within a few inches of another host. And in the meantime if the flea is to remain active enough to jump and bite it must have suitable weather, warm but not hot, moist but not wet. On the whole, nature seems to have tried hard to keep plague away from man; otherwise the human race might long ago have perished.

But the scientist in the laboratory can short-circuit this elaborate process and accomplish more quickly and more surely the job of producing plague infection by simply injecting under a rat's skin, with a syringe, a few plague bacilli taken from a culture. This artifice is more uniformly effective than the natural process precisely because plague bacilli grow better in cultures than in the complicated flea and because the syringe, guided by the human hand and brain, is more direct and efficacious than the flea and less subject to the influence of unfavorable weather.

BW could avoid the need of bacteriology right side up to reproduce the natural picture of disease; its malignant purpose, in fact, would be *more* aptly served if its weapons elicited effects very different from natural disease, the better to aggravate problems of defense and to terrorize its victims. Unlike public health, which must cope with diseases as they exist, BW could pick and choose. It could avoid the more temperamental and sensitive disease agents and could select those most likely to work. In this way some of the most formidable obstacles to progress in public health could be swept aside. Men have swallowed cultures of the germ of cholera without developing serious illness. It is characteristic of cerebrospinal meningitis that many persons harbor the causative agent in their throats without being sick. Poliomyelitis attacks only a few per thousand in any exposed population. Unless the reasons for the peculiar behavior of these diseases could be determined and the difficulties overcome by public-health research, BW could afford to stay away from them. For there are still plenty of disease agents that are not so particular; they produce disease in animals regularly and easily, and they infect man so eagerly that few laboratories will have them around, because scientists who work with them often get infected despite elaborate precautions.

Bacteria would be used in warfare not only to infect individuals but deliberately to provoke outbreaks and epidemics of disease. As a matter of principle it is harder to deal with crowds or herds than with single units. When natural science passes from the individual to the population its problems become much more complex; and unless one is prepared to stand on his head it might seem impossible for BW to make any progress in this direction at all. But let us stand on our heads, remembering that most of our values are inverted in war as a matter of course.

The study of disease in populations is more intricate than the study of disease in individuals, just as sociology is more involved than biology. It is significant that biology is accepted as a science, while the scientific status of sociology is more controversial. Biology, of which bacteriology is a part, deals with the complicated interrelationships of the elements with the whole of life. Infection is more complex in that it is a relationship of one whole with another, of host with parasite. More strictly one whole and one population (or more than one) are concerned in infection, since a very large number of individuals of the parasite species are present sooner or later in any one host. The science of epidemiology, the study of diseases in crowds, is still more complicated in that two or more populations are concerned, each made up of complex individuals which interact both with one another and as groups.

The epidemiologist's problem is a difficult one, and he can seldom operate as does the scientist in a more limited field. For example, the epidemiologist seldom experiments. More often he is a detective following clues to a source of infection or a compiler and tabulator of vital statistics.

But again the corresponding problem for BW is simplified. Imagine an inhabitant of another world, equipped if you please with a science as advanced as ours but based on a different evolution, who attempted after listening to the music of an earthly symphony orchestra to reconstruct its component instruments. He might find such an undertaking impossible. Yet if his knowledge of the physics of sound were as complete as ours, it would probably be fairly easy for him to reproduce the music faithfully with entirely different instruments. Synthesis would be much easier than analysis.

The synthesis of epidemics would also be easier than their analysis, particularly if it were neither necessary nor desirable that the artificial product resemble that of nature. If the experimental epidemiologist carefully chooses his infective agents, his animal subjects, and his experimental conditions, he can produce epidemics almost as easily as the bacteriologist can produce individual infections. Epidemics in experimental animals have been produced repeatedly, although less often than you might suppose—but only because such experiments are expensive and laborious, and the resulting disease, being rather different from any natural epidemic of man, returns limited information to public health. But the fact is significant that, given adequate funds, space, and assistance the epidemiologist can do the job with ease. There is no reason to doubt that under the impetus of war BW could do as well with human subjects as the epidemiologist does with experimental animals. To be sure, it would be necessary to choose the infective agents carefully, to determine their behavior under small-scale experimental conditions, and to select the conditions suitable for the agent and for the military purpose in hand. The possibilities open to BW would be by no means unlimited, but they would be very wide indeed.

Suppose a limited BW effect were desired, with little or no spread from victim to victim. The blinding, choking paralysis called "botulism" might be just the thing. The causative agent of this disease is an extraordinarily powerful poison called "botulinus toxin," which can be produced in test tubes, bottles, or tanks in which a bacillus called *Clostridium botulinum* is encouraged to grow. If this toxin were used in BW, primary cases of the disease might occur beyond the target area and over a limited period of time, while active toxin, persisting in the environment, was carried from place to place in water or air, in food, or on inanimate objects. This could not go on for long because the toxin is easily destroyed. What is significant here is that no infection is involved in botulism. The disease is a form of poisoning. One case does not lead to another, for the toxin does not propagate itself as bacteria do. Hence there could be no secondary cases and no epidemic.

The same is likely to be true with certain infections, although the assurance that any such would remain self-limited could never be so complete. The bacteria that cause brucellosis, or undulant fever,* for instance, would probably not give rise to secondary cases in man unless the disease appeared in the midst of such extreme devastation that even elementary sanitary safeguards were lost. This germ is highly infective for man and can cause disease by contact with the skin, by being swallowed in water or food, or by being inhaled. We usually get it from the unpasteurized milk of infected cows or goats. It is communicated readily among farm animals but not among human beings, apparently because the nature of the disease in man and his social habits combine to prevent serious contamination of the environment with the bacilli. Brucellosis, for instance, rarely produces disease of the lungs, so that the bacterium is not expelled in coughing and sneezing and therefore is not conveyed from man to man through the air. When it infects man by inhalation it comes from something other than a previous human case of the disease.

BW strategists might decide on a disease that would spread somewhat but not too much. There are agents that may be expected to do just this; although, again, under wartime conditions the results might not be quite as anticipated. The bacterium of tularemia,† or rabbit fever, like that of brucel-

---

* The fever undulates—rises and falls through a series of attacks. This happens in severe cases, along with other symptoms so varied—including, for example, melancholia and other nervous disturbances—as to make this a very difficult diagnostic problem. Laboratory methods of diagnosis are also imperfect. Brucellosis seldom kills, but its victims are often seriously ill for a month or more and then convalesce over several additional months or have repeated attacks over several years. For treatment, the sulfonamide drugs, penicillin, and streptomycin have little value separately, but a combination of sulfadiazine and streptomycin has given promising results, mainly in the milder bovine variety of brucellosis. More recently aureomycin has been tried and looks hopeful.

† Named for Tulare County, California, where nature smiles without prejudice on man, animals, insects, and bacteria and where this disease was first recognized, in 1911, as something new. The severest kind of tularemia is aptly described as "typhoidal." It resembles typhoid in that the fever is prolonged and continuous and convalescence slow. But unlike typhoid fever, tularemia yields to streptomycin.

losis, is highly infective for man and capable of infecting him by an even wider range of routes. The disease can be acquired by contact, by taking contaminated food or drinking water, by inhalation, and through the bites of many different kinds of insects. In nature it is not communicated from man to man for reasons we can only guess at. It does not have a definitive cycle of infection like bubonic plague, which in certain other respects it resembles. Perhaps because it can be carried in so many wild-animal species and by so many different insects it never finds itself, like the plague bacillus after the rats have died, with nowhere to go but to man. But a pneumonia is common in tularemia, and if the air were used as the vehicle for a BW attack with this germ, many lung infections would probably result. Yet even here (this time unlike the *pneumonic* form of plague, of which more in a moment), there is little coughing and few germs in the scanty sputum; so that while it seems to take only a few germs to infect man, not enough reach the air under natural conditions to produce secondary cases. Under BW conditions, if the dosage were massive and the concentration of primary cases high, some spread would be expected, but it would probably not be extensive.

A tropical disease called "dengue," or "breakbone fever," might be spread, in or with its mosquito carrier if need be, under conditions such that the resulting epidemic would terminate with a foreseeable change of weather. This disease has been described as temporarily the most incapacitating, although the least fatal, of epidemic diseases. Le Renard, a prewar French writer on bacterial warfare, actually suggested that its use as a weapon would be "more humanitarian" than others. The victim would merely have from two to four days of violent and crippling pains in his bones and joints and would then suffer no more than neuralgic pains, weakness, and mental depression during the subsequent months while he was getting better. Dengue is carried by the *Aëdes aegypti* mosquito which also carries yellow fever. It has been known to spread rapidly through virtually the whole of a locality; but as soon as the outside temperature drops below 59° Fahrenheit the mosquitoes stop breeding and the epidemic comes to an end. Accordingly, in appropriate terrain and with the help of moderately long-range meteorology, dengue might be used in warfare with a fair expectation that it would spread just about so far, do just about so much damage, and then stop.

At the other extreme, certain military operations might permit the use of agents of unlimited capacity for self-propagation. If an American-Russian war were in progress and particularly if things were getting tough for either side, do you suppose that either we or the Russians would hesitate to use against the other, say, pneumonic plague? This is the worst form of the great Black Death of Boccaccio's Florence. Until recently it was invariably fatal. Sulfadiazine may now cure it if enough is given before the disease makes too much headway. Pneumonic plague is seldom seen in civilized parts of the world now, but only because of the unremitting exclusion of the plague bacillus by public-health services at seaports and airports. Once it got in, crowds and cold weather would probably be the only conditions it would need to get started, and nobody knows how far it might go. The Russians, even in desperation, might keep the chance of backfiring in mind and might insulate themselves with land as well as water by aiming the plague spark at, perhaps, Minneapolis. We might pick a city in mid-Siberia, like Tobolsk.

These are examples from diseases as we know them. They are a selection of likely candidates for BW, but only a selection. There are diseases you may never have heard of, like Rift Valley fever or melioidosis. If BW came it might see diseases spread that even bacteriologists and public-health workers had never heard of. These might be newly discovered viruses or rickettsiae, of which, it is generally agreed, many remain to be found. Or they might be old germs in disguise, modified by changing their diet, by growing them on unfamiliar mediums, or by transferring them in a series through an unusual animal species. Bacteria might also be changed intrinsically by any of several fascinating new techniques that are now emerging.* And, finally, there are almost endless possibilities for extending the military imagination in combinations of germs with poisons and of germs with other germs. We shall learn much more about them, I fear, if we all stand on our heads.

Standing on his head, the bacteriologist at war could bypass the obstacles to natural public-health research. He could short-circuit the complicated cycles of infection in nature. He could select agents most likely to produce disease in the intended victim, whether it be man, animal, or crop. He could eliminate those agents and diseases that need a lot of help from nature or overcomplicated conditions or whose pattern of infection is insufficiently understood. But above all he could seize upon and make use of any known property of an agent that might be of value to BW, however rare or artificial it might be and even though it were of no known significance in public health.

For example, he might disseminate through the air breathed by an enemy crowd disease agents which *can* spread this way but seldom or never do so. Certain serious diseases, but for human intervention, would be carried only

---

* It is now possible to alter the hereditary constitution of bacteria so as to produce new types by what amounts to a marriage of different kinds, just as new varieties of dogs and wheat can be produced by crossbreeding. So far only varieties of the harmless colon bacillus, which we all have in our intestines, have been dealt with in this way, but who knows what tomorrow may bring? A relatively old trick, moreover, whereby one kind of pneumococcus can be changed to another, has now been put on a sound chemical basis. Such increased fundamental knowledge may help BW as well as public health.

by insects. But when scientists learn to accumulate large masses of the agents of these diseases in cultures, the germs strike through the air to infect those who work with them. These are among a larger group of bacteria, rickettsiae, and viruses that are distinctively dangerous to laboratory workers.

The story of accidental laboratory infections is very important to BW. It provides clues to at least two properties of disease agents that give them special value as weapons: high infectivity for man and the ability to cause infection when inhaled into the lungs.

To take the second point first, it is by now fairly well established that nearly all the notorious agents of laboratory infections can be spread through the air so as to infect man. The most common of these diseases have been glanders, tularemia, brucellosis, typhus, and other rickettsial diseases, yellow fever, psittacosis, and several other virus diseases. Among these only psittacosis ("parrot fever," a severe and frequently fatal pneumonia) uses the air-borne route exclusively. Tularemia and brucellosis are disseminated through the air elsewhere than in laboratories, probably not so rarely as textbooks suggest; but most natural infections take place by other routes. The same may have been true of glanders when this disease was commoner in both horses and men than it is now. The suggestion has been made that typhus, whose capacity for air-borne spread was recognized only very recently, may get around this way, perhaps by the drying of infected louse excrement, which may then be raised and scattered by air currents and inhaled.

No such suggestion has been offered for yellow fever. Everybody knows that yellow fever is a mosquito-borne disease. The exploits of Walter Reed and his stouthearted colleagues in Cuba at the turn of the century form one of the best-known stories of science; and the Panama Canal, which could be built only after yellow fever was conquered, is their monument. Although much more has been learned about yellow fever since then, there is still no reason to doubt that you can avoid it if you stay away from mosquitoes—unless you go into a laboratory where the virus is being worked with.

Even in laboratories, today, a good yellow-fever vaccine has closed the book of laboratory infections with this disease. Before there was a vaccine there were 34 recorded cases of yellow fever and 5 deaths among scientists who worked with the virus. Most of these cases clearly had nothing to do with mosquitoes. Some were in researchers who had handled the cultivated virus in dry powdered form. Three followed a single known exposure to the virus, and in one of these the victim had been in the laboratory on one day only and had done nothing but assist in the handling of virus preparations for a few minutes. This is a familiar pattern in the story of laboratory infections with this whole group of agents. It means that yellow-fever virus has the two attributes of the group: air transmissibility and high infectivity for man.

But yellow fever is not a respiratory disease. A person who suffers from it does not cough or sneeze and therefore, unless the scientist intervenes with his cultures, the virus never gets into the air. In nature yellow fever is strictly mosquito-borne. Its apparent air transmissibility is highly artificial and seems to have no significance. The idea of air-borne yellow fever has therefore been all but forgotten—by public-health workers. The bacteriologist upside down, however, sees this idea fresh and ominous. It means the possibility of spreading yellow-fever virus through the air, not as the tropical disease familiar to public-health workers but in temperate and cold climates where respiratory illness flourishes. It becomes possible artificially to by-pass the weakest link in the epidemic chain for this disease—the mosquito and its exacting climatic requirements. It would doubtless be difficult to start a mosquito-borne epidemic of yellow fever, but eliminate the mosquito and most of the difficulty goes with it. The whole world could be vaccinated, perhaps. I doubt that it would be.

Infectivity for man, the second lesson from laboratory infections, is a relatively new idea in bacteriology, which has only begun to mature as a quantitative science. We shall have more to say about infectivity in Chaps. 6 and 7. It is the capacity of a disease agent to infect, in terms of numbers of bacteria or concentration of virus required to cause disease or death under specified conditions. Even for experimental animals precise information on infectivity is not plentiful, while for man there is very little. But high infectivity is an extremely important property of BW agents. BW development therefore requires that as much as possible be learned about it. For plant and animal diseases it can be determined directly, but for man only indirect channels of information are open. The most useful source is accidental laboratory infections. When such infections appear in numbers in any given laboratory, assuming the customary technical competence and care, they point to high infectivity for man on the part of the disease agent implicated. Just how high can rarely be told from written records, partly because bacteriologists have not been sensitized to the idea of quantitative infectivity. A few exceptions will appear later. But it is a safe bet that any infective agent which can be handled in laboratory animals and cultures without infecting its handlers does not have the high infectivity that BW requires. I do not speak here of accidents like pricking the skin with a contaminated knife or needle. Events of this kind are dangerous with many germs of only middling infectivity. Accidental infections following needle or knife pricks or the bites of infected insects have been common with such germs as the streptococci of blood poisoning and have been recorded for many others. They represent a price that any medical bacteriologist may pay for clumsiness or carelessness; otherwise he can and does work with these germs year in and year out without getting sick. But with the bacteria of brucellosis and tularemia or the virus of psittacosis no prick or bite or other obvious accident is necessary. Shaking a bottle of culture or pouring a culture from one bottle into another may be enough to do the trick. Such simple operations raise enough fine spray to cause infection by inhalation if the germ is very potent. The high-speed food mixer ("blender"), which you may have in your kitchen and which is used in most virus laboratories to make homogenized mashes of infected materials, throws up an imperceptible but very real spray and has probably caused more laboratory infections than any other single instrument except a carelessly handled syringe. The spray is usually invisible, and the amount inhaled may be unbelievably small. It is this sort of thing that accounts for the statements frequently reiterated in reports of laboratory infections—that the patient merely walked through the laboratory without handling anything, only to come down a little later with brucellosis or one of the other diseases in the notorious list.

The agents on the list are all highly infective for man and are in consequence important in BW. It is of passing interest that many laboratory infections were reported from Camp Detrick.*

* The Merck Report mentioned some 60. Technical reports have since described 25 cases of skin anthrax, 17 cases of brucellosis, 7 of tularemia, 6 of glanders, and 1 of psittacosis. Many of these were serious, but none was fatal, no doubt in part because of the opportunities for very early diagnosis and treatment and certainly also because of conscientious medical care.

5. THE SCOPE OF BW

Late in May, 1946, the AP wires carried a story from Washington about "a germ spray capable of wiping out large cities and entire crops at a single blow," a secret weapon "far more deadly than the atomic bomb," able to destroy "all forms of life in a large city," "a germ proposition ... sprayed from airplanes that can fly high enough while doing it to be reasonably safe from ground fire," "quick and certain death." This information had "leaked" to the press through certain members of the House Appropriations Committee after closed hearings on the Navy's $4,639,718,000 appropriation bill, which was promptly passed by the House. The same afternoon another AP dispatch neatly canceled the earlier one by stating that "no such germ or bacteria or virus" exists that can wipe out all forms of life in a large city, "nor is there any known aggregation of death dealing germs of different disease kinds that can wipe out all life." *Time*, in commenting on this episode later, evidently found the disclaimer unconvincing. It suggested that there might be "a fair chance that the Congressmen's scuttlebutt was based on well-hidden fact" and offered the gloomy prediction for a nation using germ warfare that, "if all went well, its territory would be left an island of health in a world of poisonous corpses."

The AP was right the second time. There is no single biological agent and no combination or mixture of such agents that I can imagine capable of wiping out all forms of life in any area, large or small; and, as we shall see, the idea of "quick and certain death" can be associated with BW only by the grossly misinformed. There have been competent bacteriologists who would dismiss BW altogether as impracticable, but only because they have failed to appreciate its distinctive principles. Distortion or exaggeration of the potentialities of BW feeds the skepticism of these persons and confuses the whole issue both directly and through their doubts, which the uninformed take to be well founded. Such inflated claims therefore do us all a disservice, however useful they may be in pushing appropriation bills through Congress.

The scope of BW is wide but not unlimited. There are limits to the variety of its victims and to the kind of effect that can be expected from it. These limits are not precise or immovable, but there is no doubt that they exist.

The first limit depends on infective agents as parasites. A parasite must have a host to live on, and is usually so highly adapted to a particular kind of host that it can't survive with any very different kind. Some germs are sticklers for a single host species; others are more promiscuous; but none ever comes anywhere near having a range of hosts as wide as the whole living world. It is very rare, indeed, for any parasite to be able to cross the barrier between animal and plant kingdoms. I know of only two reported exceptions to this rule. One is a fungus called *Sporotrichum schenckii*, which causes disease in man and animals, mainly in the skin, and has also been thought to be capable of infecting barberry thorns and carnation buds; but that idea has been disputed. The other is a bacterium causing a leaf-spot disease of tobacco which is also infective for guinea pigs, rabbits, and mice. This germ is believed to be identical with one called *Bacillus pyocyaneus*, which sometimes causes wound infections in man and, more rarely, serious infections in old persons. Neither of these germs seems to have BW potentialities.

The most important if not the only intended victims of BW would be man and those animals and plants that are useful to man as food, as beasts of burden, or as sources of other useful products. Man would always be the ultimate victim, whether he were attacked directly or indirectly. Attempts might be made to attack him through intermediate hosts like insects, rodents, or birds; but the more direct methods are generally simpler and more predictable in their effects, and the list of such direct methods seems long enough to extend the powers of the most imaginative strategist, who would probably exhaust the easier means before he tried the harder ones. If we limit ourselves, therefore, except for incidental notice, to man and the animal and plant species upon which he depends directly and to disease agents that might conceivably be used in BW—anticipating the next chapter a little—we shall pare our subject down to workable dimensions without excessively oversimplifying it.

Within these terms there is a long list of diseases of possible significance in BW which affect, for practical purposes, only the human species. As you will by now have come to expect, it includes both familiar and unfamiliar names; and we find represented in it all the important groups of infective agents. Among bacterial diseases, for instance, are tularemia, plague, and melioidosis, and, of less probable significance in BW but worth mentioning, cerebrospinal meningitis, cholera, typhoid and related fevers, and the bacillary dysenteries. There are two spirochetal * diseases—relapsing fever and a form of

---

* The spirochetes (see the figure on p. 22) are usually listed among the bacteria, but are sometimes thought of as intermediate between the true bacteria and the one-celled animals, or protozoa; hence, in the somewhat vain hope of avoiding offense to any possible classifier, I list them separately. They look like tiny corkscrews (just the screwy part), and they bend and wriggle actively. Relatively harmless kinds of spirochetes can be found in almost anybody's mouth, sometimes in such abundance and such furious tur-

infective jaundice known as "Weil's disease"—both of somewhat doubtful value for BW. The protozoa are represented by malaria; the rickettsiae by typhus fever, scrub typhus, and Rocky Mountain spotted fever; the viruses by psittacosis, yellow fever, dengue, and some others of primary BW interest and by a more doubtful group including influenza, measles, mumps, and infantile paralysis. Add a disease due to a fungus, coccidioidomycosis, somewhat more easily pronounced as San Joaquin Valley fever.

Heading this list with tularemia may raise some educated eyebrows, for tularemia is notoriously a disease with an extraordinarily wide host range, including many species of rodents, insects, and ticks in addition to man. Except for the rabbit, however, which has minor significance as a food for man and a means toward warmth and beauty for his wife, none of these species falls within the frame of reference we have laid down. The rabbit, moreover, is a natural "reservoir" of tularemia—which is to say that rabbits are widely infected without human intervention; and it is unlikely either that they would be attacked with BW or that infection among them would increase to an economically significant degree as the result of an attack with tularemia upon man. Like the others in the list, then, tularemia, if used in BW, would be intended to infect only human victims.

There are diseases of interest to the BW strategist which affect only certain animals useful to man. Among these are the cattle diseases—rinderpest and foot-and-mouth (or "hoof-and-mouth") disease—caused by viruses; and, in the less probable category, a bacterial disease known as "hemorrhagic septicemia" (related to plague in man) and a disease called "pleuropneumonia," due to a peculiar little microbe that doesn't classify easily.* There is also a virus disease of swine,

moil as might astonish you. The best known spirochete is called *Treponema pallidum* and is the cause of syphilis.

* See the figure on p. 21.

called "hog cholera," and at least two virus diseases of poultry, known as "fowl plague" and "Newcastle disease."

Beyond this are a few diseases that affect both man and certain useful animals, whose agents might be used in BW for attack on either or both. This category is occupied chiefly by three bacterial diseases: anthrax, which can infect cattle, sheep, pigs, goats, horses, camels, and other animals as well as man; glanders, found mainly in horses, mules, and asses but transmissible to man; and brucellosis, or Bang's disease, different varieties of which attack cattle, swine, and goats, man being susceptible to all but with particular severity to the swine and goat varieties. Two virus diseases are also worth mentioning here, one affecting sheep, cattle, goats, and man and called "Rift Valley * fever," and the other horses and man, known as "equine encephalomyelitis." Finally we ought to mention botulism, different types of which affect horses, cattle, sheep, and poultry as well as man.

The different botulinus toxins, as I have pointed out, are not infective agents but chemical substances (proteins). Two of them, known as types A and B, were isolated in pure form during the war by scientists at Camp Detrick. These would be agents of chemical rather than biological warfare except that they can be made only by biological processes. The bacillus called *Clostridium botulinum* (types of which correspond to the different toxins) manufactures them as it grows in appropriate nutritive broths. We can't make them chemically, just as, thus far, chemists have been unable to

---

* Rift Valley fever was first recognized in 1930 as a new virus disease of sheep on a farm north of Lake Naivasha in the great Rift Valley of East Africa. The virus is highly infective for sheep and man. More than 90 per cent of infected newborn lambs die, but in man the disease resembles dengue or influenza, with a brief period of fever and severe incapacitating pains in joints or abdomen, nearly always followed by recovery. Almost every native herder in the original outbreak acquired the disease, as has almost every laboratory worker who has handled the virus. Little is known about its means of transmission in nature, but the record leaves little doubt that it could be air-borne.

synthesize any other true protein. The botulinus toxins produce disease only by acting as poisons and not as infective agents; in other words, they do not multiply in the host. But they resemble infective agents rather than poisons in that they affect only a few host species.

When we come to the plants, we find that the best known antiplant agents associated with BW are pure synthetic chemical substances—the plant "hormones," or growth regulators, which were tested and reported on at length by Camp Detrick scientists. Of more than a thousand such compounds tested one, 2,4-dichlorophenoxyacetic acid, has now become familiar to householders all over the world as 2,4-D, the weed killer. This substance, when used in proper concentration, has a selective action on broad-leaf plants. Another group of compounds, the phenylcarbamates, is more active against grass seedlings and cereals. But these are not BW agents except by courtesy. They happen to have been investigated by BW scientists at Camp Detrick. They differ sharply from infective agents and even from the botulinus toxins in that they owe what selectivity they have entirely to concentration effects. In sufficiently high concentration they are capable of killing plants indiscriminately, just as a poison like potassium cyanide is capable of killing any living thing that breathes.

There is little public information on true infective agents of plants that may be useful in BW. There are diseases of plants caused by special kinds of bacteria, by particular viruses, and by fungi; and we need not doubt that among these the scientist standing on his head may find agents to suit the purposes of BW. Three such have been mentioned in technical reports from Camp Detrick. All three are fungus diseases, two affecting rice ("blast" disease and "brown-spot" disease), and one causing "late blight" of potatoes and tomatoes. Late blight is the disease that ruined the potato crop in Ireland in 1845; the resulting severe famine caused the emigration of hundreds of thousands of Irish to the United States and forced the British parliament to repeal the Corn Laws and begin a policy of free trade.

It is plain that BW is distinctive among forms of warfare in its requirement that the weapon be not merely aimed at the target but also suited for it. If the intended victim is man, the agent must be capable of affecting man, and likewise for particular kinds of animals and plants. There is no reason to believe that a cow would be inconvenienced if it found itself in the midst of a cloud of tularemia bacilli sufficiently concentrated to infect every man who breathed it. Nor would a man be likely to suffer in any way if he ate beef from an animal with rinderpest.* The animals in a pasture heavily contaminated with the bacteria of Bang's disease or the spores of anthrax might all die rapidly, but the vegetation would not be altered, except indirectly by interference with the cycles of nature. And, conversely, the men in a rice field sprayed with *Helminthosporium oryzae,* the cause of the brown-spot disease, could touch, eat, or inhale this fungus without being affected by it except through loss of their harvest.

So much for the first limit to the scope of BW—the limiting range of host or victim species. There are also limits to the effects that can be anticipated. As a general principle, BW is unlikely ever to kill *all* its target victims, even within the intended biological class, and BW will certainly never act instantaneously, like high explosive or an atomic bomb. The symptoms of infection do not begin to appear until the incubation period has passed; that is, it usually takes from

---

* This may sound shocking, but there is no reason to doubt it, since there has never been any evidence of rinderpest infection of man despite abundant opportunity for it. If a steer with rinderpest were slaughtered and its carcass dressed and prepared like healthy beef it could probably be used safely as human food. Men might reject it, but for aesthetic rather than for scientific reasons. I would probably have to be pretty hungry myself before I'd eat it.

several days to several weeks or more, after the germ has entered the body, before the infected individual becomes sick. Hence the idea of "quick and certain death" from BW is distinctly out of order.

Variability is one of the fundamental properties of all things and processes biological. Infective disease is a biological process and is subject to variation in all its characteristics and end results. In nature there have occasionally been diseases that have killed all their victims with few or no exceptions, like rabies (once the disease has actually started) or pneumonic plague; but even these are disappearing as absolutes under the influence of modern treatment. Experimentally, there are some invariably fatal infections, and it is practicable as a general rule to infect laboratory animals with so large a dose of agent that 100 per cent of exposed animals are uniformly killed. But the conditions of such experiments are more artificial or, if you will, more subject to experimental control than could ever be expected in practical biological warfare. BW may carry a high probability of death, but never a certainty.

Variability applies not only to the end result of infection—death or recovery—but also to infection itself. In nature it is almost inevitable that in any outbreak of infection among a population—whether of men, animals, or plants—some individuals, few or many, will escape. They may escape because they avoid contact with the infecting agent or with a sufficient dose of it, or because they have a sufficient degree of natural resistance to the agent or have previously recovered from the disease or have been vaccinated against it; or there may be a combination of such reasons. It is not difficult under strictly controlled experimental conditions to overcome any or all of these protective factors and to expose laboratory animals to amounts of infecting agent sufficient to infect them all, uniformly; but no such absolute result could ever be predicted under the more complicated conditions of the field.

BW could never be absolute in its effects. It could not be expected to infect all the individual intended victims in the target area, much less to kill them. Just what might we expect it to do?

The most diverse effects could be expected—and to a considerable extent they could be predicted by the attackers —probably with sufficient accuracy for military purposes. The character of the effect would depend largely upon the nature of the agent used, partly on the way in which it was used. Effects on the individual human victim might be chosen in such a way as to differ in kind as well as in degree. Some agents, like botulinus toxin or the bacilli of plague, would produce a relatively high proportion of deaths. Others, like the germs of tularemia or brucellosis, might yield relatively few deaths but wholesale incapacitation for long periods. In judging the military effectiveness of a weapon, military men consider incapacitation preferable to killing, since the sick tie up medical personnel and hospital facilities and otherwise drain the resources and impede the movements of the force that must care for them. Until World War II, naturally occurring epidemic diseases were always more to be feared by armies than the bullets of the enemy. In recent years, improvement of high explosive weapons, even without the atomic bomb, and major advances in both prevention and treatment of disease have combined to make war more destructive than germs. BW threatens to reverse this trend.

BW might also be used deliberately with the expectation that only a few casualties could spread terror and demoralization. A handful of cases of a rare disease with dreadful potentialities, like melioidosis,* psittacosis, or cold-weather

---

* So far as anybody knows, melioidosis is an exceedingly rare disease, with potentialities that seem abundantly dreadful. Up to 1938 there had been re-

(air-borne) yellow fever, occurring in a large population center, might completely disorganize the community in wartime, what with the implication of BW and the threat of successive attacks. Not long ago the whole country watched while New York City was alerted to an epidemic threat.

On February 24, 1947, a forty-seven-year-old American businessman left Mexico City and traveled by bus to New York, after having lived in Mexico for six years. That evening he had a headache and a pain in the back of his neck, and two days later he had a rash. When he arrived in the city on March 1 and registered at a midtown hotel, he was not too ill to do a little sight-seeing and to walk through a large department store; the epidemiological detectives subsequently retraced his steps with some care. On March 10 he died in the city hospital for contagious diseases, with the doctors disagreeing as to what had been wrong with him. But when a twenty-seven-year-old man and a twenty-two-month-old baby girl who had been discharged from this hospital both returned with what looked like chicken pox, two outside authorities were called in to set the matter straight. They diagnosed the disease as smallpox, and only then was it found that slices of the skin from the ill-fated bus rider showed him to have died of smallpox as well. The twenty-seven-year-old man infected his wife, who died, and three others. Of two additional cases that developed at the city hospital, one did not show signs of smallpox until he had reached a convales-

---

corded a world total of 95 cases, 90 of which had been fatal. All 95 had been observed in a limited area of the Far East, including the Malay Archipelago and neighboring parts of Indo-China, Burma, and India. Since then the number of recorded cases has risen to about 300, including several in American soldiers during the war. Nearly all have died in spite of modern treatment in the most recent cases. The bacillus of melioidosis, *Malleomyces pseudomallei*, is a close relative of the germ of glanders, and the disease itself is like glanders but worse. It does not come to man from horses but probably from rats. The rat flea which transmits plague can also carry melioidosis. There is no evidence that melioidosis is ever air-borne in nature, but animals can easily be infected with the germ by inhalation. (See the figure on p. 65.)

cent home at Milbrook, New Jersey; there he was responsible for three additional cases.

There were 12 cases in all, and 2 deaths. But the outbreak seemed so serious that the local health officers and the city administration, with the help of press and radio, induced more than 6,350,000 persons to be vaccinated in less than a month; hundreds of thousands stood in line for many hours for this purpose; the United States Public Health Service explored possible epidemic contacts in 29 states; the whole country took notice; and *Life* did a picture story on the outbreak. Dr. Weinstein, city Health Commissioner, said that such an outbreak "could be a major catastrophe. . . . In 1901, an epidemic of smallpox in New York City resulted in 1,955 cases and 410 deaths. Had the same rate prevailed in the 1947 outbreak there would have been 4,310 cases and 902 deaths." But 12 cases were enough to alert the world's largest city. Suppose we had been at war and that at least one well established BW attack had occurred previously. . . .

The enemy would probably aim to produce more than a single initial case of infection, and if there were many some would doubtless be widely scattered before their symptoms appeared. But twelve cases of illness in a population of seven and a half million might be enough in wartime. It could be equivalent to a major battle with conventional weapons.

So much, for the present, for BW directed against man. In animals and plants, BW would be a form of economic warfare, aimed principally at the food supply, secondarily at leather, wool, cotton, and any number of other biological products. It would be long-range warfare almost exclusively, since its effects would be rather slow in appearing and would not influence reserve stocks. But again it would divert enemy activity toward defensive and reparative measures, and again it would have psychological implications that might be hardly less important than its frankly destructive effects. If such warfare against either animals or plants or both were sufficiently extensive and successful, an additional long-range effect might be counted among the most disastrous consequences of BW—disturbance of the cycles of nature. Animals (including man) depend ultimately on plants for their food supply, and plants depend on animals to fertilize the soil. Any extensive destruction of either, sufficient to upset the balance of nature, would in time react upon both. Thus the process of desert formation, to which man has already contributed by thoughtless deforestation and improper methods of farming, might be accelerated by the destructive effects of biological agents on animals and plants.

According to Major General Alden H. Waitt, the "ideal" weapon was characterized many years ago as one which, in addition to other properties, would "inflict no permanent damage upon property." It seems that man tends to regenerate his kind with little outside aid, whereas enemy property, when enough of it has been destroyed, must be repaired or replaced by the victor nation, a requirement which adds heavily to the cost of victory. Gas warfare was thought of as such an "ideal" weapon, but evidently did not justify early hopes, since, although it had been highly developed, it was not used in World War II. (The reason or reasons why chemical warfare was not used in the recent war, by the way, have never to my knowledge been made public. I assume that they were strictly military rather than humanitarian. And since BW is now under development in this country under the auspices of the United States Chemical Corps, or erstwhile Chemical Warfare Service, I assume further that the objections to CW do not apply to BW.) Perhaps BW has now become the "ideal" weapon. Indications are that it could be used to destroy or incapacitate human beings without destroying property. This is one of several important respects in which it differs from the atomic bomb.

6. WHAT IS A BW AGENT?

IF bacteriology is to be turned upside down and made to serve the destructive ends of war, the infective agents that will be its weapons must be chosen shrewdly. The choice will not be easy. Only trial and success in battle can justify it completely, but this is impossible if BW is to be made ready for impending war; yet no other method of selection can give more than provisional information. The BW strategist will know that not all germs lend themselves to BW. He will do his best to find out which ones can be rejected out of hand and which are to be selected—with, no doubt, a questionable group in the middle. He will have to do this first by reasoning about it. Then he will test his judgment as best he can in laboratory and field, confirming his choice and modifying it as he goes along. If he works well he will end with a batch of weapons that seem dependable, but he cannot be sure until they are tried in war.

If BW is to be made practicable, then, a working answer must be found to the question: What distinguishes a potential BW agent from just any germ? We do not know exactly how this question will be answered by BW strategists; there may be more than one way of answering it. But we have an answer that will serve our purpose of understanding BW. It is given in the 1942 Report, upon which we depend for basic principles of BW. There ten criteria for the selection and application of BW agents are listed and briefly defined, and

WHAT IS A BW AGENT?

most of the Report is devoted to the measurement of individual infective agents against them. In the original terminology and order they are: (1) infectivity; (2) casualty effectiveness; (3) availability; (4) resistance; (5) means of transmission; (6) epidemicity; (7) specific immunization; (8) therapy; (9) detection; and (10) retroactivity. Let us look at them in sequence.

By the first criterion, *infectivity,* we mean the capacity of a given kind of germ to produce infection, as compared with other kinds. For the most part this refers to a quantity—to the number of germs required to produce infection (or death) under a given set of conditions. It seems important that disease agents selected for BW be highly infective, that is, that the number of individual germs of the agent needed to yield a casualty in the intended victim species be very small.

The need for high infectivity is not simply a matter of economy, since germs are both small and cheap. Its importance depends on two things. First, if a BW agent is to be an effective weapon, a sufficient amount must be distributed in the target environment so that, say, each cupful of water in a reservoir or each cubic foot of air enveloping a crowd will be sufficiently loaded with the agent to infect the drinker or breather. If large spaces are to be contaminated, like a city reservoir or the air of Madison Square Garden, it becomes important for tactical reasons that the package containing the agent be small. If something the size of a blockbuster were needed, one might as well depend on the high explosive directly.

Secondly, and even more important, there seems to be an inverse relation between infectivity and the resistance of the attacked host which has in it something more than the matter of numbers of germs. If a single germ can multiply in the body, that single germ is enough to produce infection. If a million germs are necessary to do the trick, it is probably because all but a few of them are destroyed before the body's defenses are overcome; the remaining few then multiply in the weakened host. It follows that, if a single germ is enough, infection is a much more certain event than when very large numbers are required. The single germ has in it something that makes the body defenses powerless against it. When properly handled, one pair of pneumococci is enough to kill a mouse; and one bacillus of tularemia is also a killing dose for the same animal. But with the germs of cholera, even when they are artificially protected (with mucin, the substance that makes mucus thick) more than half a million are necessary to kill the same animal species.

No two living things are ever quite alike. Within every species the individuals vary. This variability applies to both germ and host in the uneasy partnership of infection—to the germ's infectivity and to the host's resistance against it. Any one instance of infection is therefore not a reliable guide to another of the same kind; infectivity cannot be measured in a single animal. Groups of animals must be used, with precise measures of infectivity dependent on averages of many trials. Even so, something more than a simple average is needed to measure infectivity.

If a single germ of any given kind is regularly enough to infect, the problem is simple; but this is not true of many kinds of germs. If appreciably more than one germ is needed, it has been shown that the way in which the host's response—infection or death in the average of many trials—varies with the number of germs used to infect follows a characteristic pattern. If a chart is made in which the numbers of animals that respond are plotted against the numbers of germs inoculated, the resulting curve looks like an italic *S* with its ends flattened. As the infecting dose is increased in successive groups of hosts, the percentage of animals infected increases at first slowly, then progressively more rapidly, then again more slowly as the point is approached at which 100 per cent of the hosts are infected. An occasional very sensitive animal becomes infected with a very small dose. As the dose

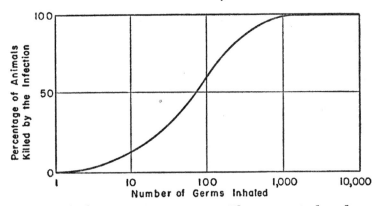

FIG. 3. A dosage-infection curve. *This curve is based on actual experiments with the germ of melioidosis and with little brown furry rodents called Syrian hamsters, 266 of which were exposed to infection by inhalation to obtain the average values for dosage and percentage killed from which the curve was drawn. Numbers of germs are given on a logarithmic scale instead of the ordinary arithmetical one so as to cover the range from 1 to 10,000. The 50 per cent fatal dose ("LD_{50}") was computed as 73.5 germs. (Based on data given in* Experimental Air-Borne Infection. *See page 114.*)

is increased the proportion of animals that responds becomes more consistent, and is most regular and dependable at the point where 50 per cent of the hosts are affected. As this point is passed the occasional very resistant animal tends to make it increasingly difficult to infect 100 per cent of the hosts. Both ends of this relationship are thus too uncertain to be useful as precise measures: the point at which one animal out of many is infected and that at which all the animals are infected. The least variable and therefore most reliable dosage value is found at the point of 50 per cent infection, where the greatest change in numbers of animals infected results if the dosage is changed in either direction. Accordingly, in precise experimental work, infectivity is defined as the number of any given kind of germ required to infect (or to kill) one-half of the exposed hosts. The definition must include all the experimental conditions; mice and rabbits are not likely to respond alike, and either kind of animal may respond differently if infected through the skin or by inhalation. It is evident that the experiments required to measure infectivity will be elaborate. Each test requires a good deal of work; but there is nothing intrinsically difficult about the job.

It should be emphasized that what is true for animals, not to mention plants, is not automatically true for man. Although infectivity tests require extensive experimentation it is easy enough to do them, so that infectivity can be determined for laboratory animals and, if necessary, for any given kind of animal or plant. But the same cannot be done for man. Precise infectivity data for man are, in fact, a practical impossibility. The Nazis performed medical experiments on human victims, and it is probably characteristic of their general depravity that their experiments, conceived in untempered cruelty, yielded no useful information.*

At all events we have no infectivity data for man that begin to compare in precision with the information available or obtainable for other host species. In the next chapter we shall examine a few infectivity values based on single instances of human infection—accidental infections. They are very crude by laboratory standards of precision, but they are the best we have or are likely to get. Otherwise our information on infectivity for man can be obtained only by a sort of guesswork,

* This point is dealt with at some length in Chap. 13.

by inference based on uncontrolled events. For example, the fact that very large numbers of human beings have been infected with and have died of bubonic plague as the result of a single fleabite, that traditionally insignificant wound, suggests that the plague bacillus is highly infective for man. The prevalence of accidental laboratory infections caused by one of a characteristic group of disease agents and the manner in which they are brought about points to high infectivity. For the most part, then, so far as man is concerned as the potential victim of BW and so far as the selection of BW agents depends on infectivity, we depend almost entirely on circumstantial evidence.

The second criterion for the selection of BW agents, *casualty effectiveness*, is hardly less important than infectivity. If the agent is to be used as a weapon it is obviously necessary that it be capable of inducing disability or damage in the attacked host. Diseases like ringworm or pyorrhea, although they are by no means trivial as public-health problems, are not suitable for BW because they do not interfere seriously or predictably with the normal activities of the person who has them. The venereal diseases can be ruled out on similar grounds, and also because they do not meet other criteria. Syphilis in particular can be a gravely incapacitating disease, but severe effects are insufficiently constant for the purposes of BW and generally occur only after the disease has run its course for several or many years. Hence its casualty effectiveness would be too low.*

---

* The psychological effects of BW have already been mentioned (Chap. 5). Such effects might include psychological casualties, and syphilis contracted through BW would probably qualify under this head. But it is highly unlikely that the spirochete of syphilis could be effectively used as a weapon; it falls down particularly with respect to the criteria of *availability* (we do not know how to grow the spirochete in cultures); *resistance* (its capacity to survive in the environment seems to be excessively low); probable *means of transmission* (in nature, syphilis is transmitted by direct contact only, probably because of the poor resistance of the spirochete when separated from the host); *therapy* (cure and prevention are now relatively easy). General

Part of the measure of the casualty effectiveness of a BW agent would lie in certain characteristics of the infection it produced. Among these would be its death rate, or "case mortality" (number of deaths per hundred cases of the illness), the relative duration of its severe or incapacitating phase, the severity and duration of the period of convalescence, and the length of its incubation period. Given a sufficient degree of incapacitation or injury to warrant selection of the agent for BW purposes, the case-mortality and duration factors would influence not selection but application—the particular tactical uses of the agent. Incubation period, on the other hand, would influence selection as well as application. Diseases like leprosy and rabies, whose incubation periods may range from many weeks to several years, would probably not be acceptable as BW agents for this reason. Speaking generally, diseases with incubation periods of not more than a few days would probably qualify best; but periods as long as two weeks or even more might not disqualify an agent that possessed other appropriate properties.

The criterion of *availability* is essentially self-evident, but some of its underlying conditions may be worth explanation. Obviously, if an agent is to be used in BW, the agent itself must be at hand, and it must be possible and practicable to prepare enough of it to meet its particular requirements. On the first point, any difficulties that may exist are products of secrecy engendered by war or preparation for war. Serious diseases are matters of world-wide concern, and it is customary for nations at peace, whether diplomatic or economic relations between them are entirely cordial or not, to exchange infective agents for purposes of research. Hence, in normal times, if any given agent is lacking in a particular

---

Leon A. Fox, in an article on BW published in 1933, offered the cogent opinion that "the soldier's danger from the venereal diseases will not come from the open, avowed wartime enemy who loves him least but from the money-loving or uniform-worshipping ladies who profess to love him most."

country, the director of a qualified laboratory or institute has only to write to a scientist elsewhere who is known to have the agent in his laboratory, whereupon he duly receives a sample of it by mail or other suitable carrier. At present, however, and as long as the threat of a major war exists, it may be taken for granted that such free interchange, like the traditional internationalism of science as a whole, will be restricted. But restrictions are likely to apply mainly to newly discovered infective agents. If such agents upon isolation are found to have properties that suggest their usefulness for BW, the agent itself and all information about it may at once be covered with the shroud of secrecy. This is not an inconsiderable possibility; but it remains true that all the agents mentioned in this book are probably available in or accessible to every civilized country on earth.

The second point—that of the practicability of preparing the agent in required amounts—poses different problems which make it a major criterion for the selection of BW agents. If relatively large quantities of the agent are required it must be possible to obtain satisfactory *cultures* of it. This can be done with the majority of infective agents but not with all; and the ease or difficulty associated with the process differs widely. Most bacteria reproduce and multiply, in cultures or large masses or in cloudy swarms, when planted in a suitable culture medium. The basis of such a medium is most commonly a clear meat broth, to which agar-agar, a pectin-like substance derived from seaweed, may be added to solidify it. Similar and equally useful mediums have been prepared from cheaper ingredients than meat, for instance, certain waste products of food processing. While many types of bacteria can be grown successfully in such simple mediums, others require the addition of special foods or even vitamins. Fungi grow as a rule on even simpler mediums.

The rickettsiae and the viruses cannot be grown by any

such means; they multiply only in the presence of suitable host cells. They can be grown in cultures of such cells or tissues, but most tissue cultures are too difficult to handle and do not provide sufficient crops of virus to be practicable for BW production. Most rickettsiae and viruses grow abundantly, however, when they are planted in developing hens' eggs under appropriate conditions; and since eggs are comparatively cheap and can be obtained and easily handled in large quantities, this procedure provides a very satisfactory method for obtaining them in large amounts.

There are nevertheless a few infective agents that cannot be cultivated by any of these means, and for the most part such germs would therefore seem to be excluded from consideration for BW. Among these are the spirochetes of syphilis and of a disease called "relapsing fever." These microbes can be kept alive in laboratories only by infecting animals with them and transferring infected tissue or blood from animal to animal. Another is the bacillus of leprosy, and still others are the viruses of German measles and chicken pox. Most of these agents would probably not be selected for BW anyway, for other reasons. It is interesting that mumps and dengue viruses, both of which have potential BW attributes, were listed as unavailable in the 1942 Report because they could not be grown. But both have been successfully cultivated since then.

The suggestion was made at that time that dengue virus and relapsing-fever spirochetes might be used in BW despite our inability to grow them by maintaining and disseminating them in their natural vectors, the virus in *Aëdes* mosquitoes and the spirochete in ticks. It is doubtful that such methods would be as serviceable militarily as those that depend on direct dispersion of larger amounts of cultivated agent; but these examples suggest that the need for cultivation, although general, may not be universal.

WHAT IS A BW AGENT?

The fourth criterion is *resistance*. Two distinct properties of infective agents are covered by this term. One is their capacity to withstand environmental influences that are in some degree destructive, like drying, the ultraviolet radiation in sunlight, high temperatures, or high concentrations of disinfectants. The second implies that they must be able to retain their capacity to infect—their virulence—under field conditions as well as in the usually more favorable environment in which they are cultured.

These are all relative matters. Infective agents have the instability characteristic of living things. They are subject to injury and often tend to lose virulence when subjected to unfavorable environments or even when cultivated in favorable mediums. But some agents are much more stable than others, and the stability even of the more fragile ones can usually be improved by laboratory manipulations. Even as delicate a germ as the bacillus of tularemia, which has been known to die off rapidly under conditions that do not seem to affect most other bacteria at all, lends itself to stabilization by such means, so that in all probability it could be used for BW purposes. The spirochete of syphilis appears to have a similar delicacy; but I think this germ, too, if it could first be cultured and then studied, might be stabilized.

Consequently resistance may not be important for the *selection* of BW agents. An agent suitable in all other respects could probably be made resistant enough if it were not so to begin with. This property would, however, modify the applications of the agent. The more resistant agents, like the very hardy spores of anthrax or the only slightly more perishable *Coccidioides* fungus, could be used to contaminate open terrain with the expectation that they would remain alive for long periods. Most other infective agents would have to be disseminated in such a way that they would pass more quickly to their intended target victims. The most sensitive ones, like the tularemia bacillus or the coccus of cerebrospinal meningitis, might be usable only by methods of direct transmission from source to victim—for instance, through the air.

An example of phenomenal resistance is given in the 1942 Report for the ordinarily unstable spirochete of relapsing fever. This germ is harbored in nature in certain species of bloodsucking ticks. Such ticks infest both man and animals but do not attack either species except to feed. They become engorged with blood in a single feeding and then do not feed again for a considerable period of time. Edward Francis, the venerable United States Public Health Service researcher,* studied ticks infected with relapsing-fever spirochetes and found that the germs remained alive and virulent in ticks that had been starved for as long as five years and that the infection could then be transmitted to a monkey by biting. He also found that other ticks infected a monkey after the ticks had been starved for four years and then infected another monkey by feeding on its blood two and a half years later.

Means of transmission and *epidemicity* (relative tendency to spread from host to host), criteria five and six, respectively, were considered at some length in Chap. 4 and need be mentioned here only briefly. These criteria bear particularly on the tactical application of BW agents, and epidemicity might not be a factor in selection at all. Means of transmission, however, would influence selection and might do so in a rather important way. A capacity for transmission via the air, particularly, would recommend an agent for BW purposes, whether such transmission were known to occur in nature or, perhaps even more significantly, if it were known that the

---

* It is interesting that this scientist, in a remarkable paper published in 1938, describes a case of accidental infection with relapsing-fever spirochetes resulting from the bites, on two successive days, of laboratory-infected ticks. The patient became ill seven days after the first bite and was very sick, having nine relapses over a total period of 111 days. It is only by a careful reading of the paper that one discovers that the patient was Edward Francis himself.

agent could be induced to pass through the air only under artificial conditions. Yellow fever and typhus fever are examples of diseases characteristically insect-borne in nature but in all probability capable of air-borne dissemination. Such knowledge would encourage the selection of these agents for BW development.

While air-borne infection looks like the most important route for large-scale BW directed particularly against man, other routes of infection are by no means excluded. Water- and food-borne agents are a doubtful group for the most part both because sanitation of water and foods is highly developed and because the agents concerned either have low infectivity or are not adequately understood; but it may well be that further research along these lines may open possibilities not now recognized. Several possible BW applications of agents transmitted only by certain insects or ticks have been mentioned—among them dengue fever or malaria in appropriate mosquitoes and relapsing fever.

The seventh and eighth criteria are *specific immunization* and *therapy*. Other things being equal, a given agent would be more or less useful than another if effective means were available to protect one's own population by vaccination against it or by either preventive or curative treatment with a potent drug or antibiotic. The virus of smallpox might not be selected because effective vaccination is available all over the world. Since this vaccine is not universally used, however, smallpox might be chosen for attack on a population known to be unprotected. It is of some interest that this applies to several of our own states.* Of course, if our enemies

* It is known that the occurrence of smallpox in the United States shows a marked inverse relationship to the varying state laws on vaccination, being lowest where vaccination is compulsory, highest where compulsory vaccination is prohibited by law, and intermediate where there is local option or in states that have no vaccination laws at all. During the four-year period 1938–1941 there were 0.8 cases of smallpox per 100,000 in the 13 (mainly eastern)

had a vaccine or a highly effective treatment for a given agent which we lacked, they might be all the more tempted to use that agent against us. In general it would be important to develop or to improve both vaccines and means of treatment for individual agents selected for BW.

The ninth criterion, *detection*, refers to the relative ease or difficulty with which an agent could be identified by the defenders of an area where it had been used in BW. Since this is an important aspect of defense against BW we shall return to it when we take up that point. The detectability of an agent is likely to modify its application in BW but to have little influence on its selection as an agent. As we shall see, the detection and identification of BW agents in actual warfare would probably be difficult—much more so than the detection of the agents of chemical warfare. While such difficulty might tend to favor selection of one agent, another would not be excluded because, like the anthrax bacillus, it was comparatively easy to identify. A particularly troublesome bacterium, like *Brucella*, might nevertheless seem a better agent because it would probably be very hard to detect.

The tenth criterion is *retroactivity*, or the capacity of an agent to backfire against those using it as a weapon. This property of infective agents has broader implications than as a criterion for their selection and application, with which we are concerned here. It will influence the major decision by a nation to use or not to use BW. Let us assume for the present that the political, geographical, and other considerations bearing on the question are such that the decision to use BW or to have it ready for use has been made. The ques-

---

states which required vaccination as a prerequisite for school attendance, as compared with a case rate of 13.2 in the states (Arizona, California, Minnesota, North Dakota, South Dakota, Utah and Washington) which had various provisions prohibiting the requirement of vaccination (Hampton, B.C., United States Public Health Reports 58: 1771, 1943).

tion is, then: To what degree will retroactivity determine which BW agents are to be selected and used?

The answer to this question will lie partly in the differences between individual agents and beyond this in the character of the war that is imminent or in progress. The two properties of agents that bear most directly on retroactivity are their infectivity and their epidemicity. The first will determine the direct danger from an agent to those who study it, develop it, produce it, and use it; the second will be of importance in relation to the possibility that epidemic disease in an attacked country may spread back to the country that used it. Since we may assume that agents will be selected for BW by virtue of their high infectivity, it follows that safe methods for handling and using them will have to be available to the handlers. This problem was met and satisfactorily solved in World War II. We have already seen that epidemicity varies widely among infective agents and that it would determine their uses in war rather than their selection as BW agents. It is likely that the whole range of epidemicity would be covered in the list of agents selected for development—from botulinus toxin, which is not infective and therefore has no self-propagating power, to the plague bacillus, which might conceivably cause a world-wide pandemic. Once such a selection had been made, it would remain necessary to determine as fully as possible the potential retroactive powers of each agent as part of its strategic and tactical evaluation. Such information, when related to the shape of the war itself, would in turn determine the relative emphasis to be placed on the development and production of individual agents.

A BW agent, then, is not just any disease-producing germ but one having a particular set of properties, which has been chosen both because it conforms with certain criteria and because it is capable of doing a predetermined military job. It will be highly infective, so that a small amount of it will go a long way. It will be capable of inducing damage, significant in kind and in amount, in its particular host victim, whether this be man, animal, or plant. It will lend itself to production in adequate quantity and will be, or will have been made, sufficiently stable to remain viable and virulent under the conditions chosen for its production and dissemination. The way or ways in which the agent is or can be disseminated so as to bring about the intended effects will be known, as will its capacity for self-propagation. Vaccines or other specific means for protection against the agent and substances having special value for treatment of the disease caused by it may or may not be available; if not, the attempt will be made to prepare them. Such means as can be devised for the rapid detection and identification of the agent will be at hand or under development. The special dangers inherent in the agent for its developers and users, both directly and at long range, will be known or studied.

And, finally, if an agent conforming with these properties has been newly discovered and its nature kept secret or if it is a variant of an old agent with new properties, perhaps including a specific vaccine with protective power only against this variant, these facts will particularly recommend it for development and use in BW.

7. POTENCY

IN the fall of 1946, Dr. Gerald Wendt, editorial director of *Science Illustrated*, made newspaper headlines with a radio story, later amplified in his magazine, which stated that a 1-inch cube of crystalline botulinus toxin, weighing about an ounce, would be enough to kill every person in the United States and Canada. He had based this statement on an account in *Science Newsletter* which attributed to Dr. Carl Lamanna of Camp Detrick the estimate that the killing dose of this poison for a 165-pound man would be roughly 0.15 gamma, 1 gamma (or microgram) being one-millionth of a gram. There are about 28 grams in an ounce.

Dr. Wendt's statement was news not only because it dramatized in spectacular fashion the extraordinary potency of this poison but because the information itself was the first postwar suggestion of the amount of damage a BW agent might cause. The day after the first newspaper story appeared, Major General Alden H. Waitt, Chief of the Army Chemical Corps, confirmed the fact that United States biological-warfare scientists at Camp Detrick had succeeded during the war "in isolating in pure form a bacterial toxin which is perhaps the most highly toxic substance known." Dr. Lamanna headed one of two groups of Camp Detrick scientists who did this job independently; and by this time the reports of both groups had appeared in technical journals.

Botulinus toxin, as we have seen, is a poisonous substance produced by a bacillus called *Clostridium botulinum*. In nature this toxin is responsible for an uncommon form of food poisoning associated with improperly preserved food. The resulting disease, called "botulism," is characterized by blurred vision and other disorders of the eyes, swelling of the tongue, dryness of the mouth, and progressively increasing weakness of the body muscles, leading to death in a high proportion of cases. The toxin, as General Waitt suggested, is probably the most active of all known poisons and is the only member of its class—true biological toxins—that is poisonous when swallowed. The others, like diphtheria or tetanus toxin or the snake venoms, must be injected into or formed in the tissues; they can be swallowed with impunity because the gastric juice destroys them. Crystalline botulinus toxin is an astonishingly powerful substance. In fact, the crystals obtained by the Abrams group at Camp Detrick, who used a different method, were even more active than those prepared by the Lamanna team.

The Abrams crystals assayed at 30 million fatal doses per milligram for the white mouse, when injected into the belly. This is 30 billion (3×10^{10}) doses per gram, or about 840 billion doses per ounce. The mice used weighed about 20 grams. A 165-pound man weighs 75 kilograms, or 75,000 grams. Assuming equal susceptibility, gram for gram, in mouse and man, 1 gram would contain about 8 million fatal doses for man, or 224 million per ounce. The estimated combined population of the United States and Canada in 1947 was 156,184,000. Add Mexico and the Caribbean area, and the total, 196,264,000, is still smaller than our estimated number of human fatal doses in one ounce of this crystalline toxin.

If arithmetic were our only guide, one ounce of pure botulinus toxin might kill more than 200 million human beings. But arithmetic, however painful it may be to some of us, is not in itself fatal; and there are good reasons to doubt that these superlatively potent crystals could in actual practice do anywhere near so much damage. But don't allow yourself to be relieved. Even if the arithmetic of botulinus toxin were in fact the whole story and there were more than 200 million potential human deaths in each ounce of it, there is good evidence that other BW agents may be *considerably more potent!*

Underneath the botulinus arithmetic lurk two assumptions for which nothing in the record gives us license. The first is that mice and men are equally susceptible to the toxin, gram for gram. Nobody knows whether this is true. There were no deaths among the human population of Camp Detrick during the war, from botulism or any other disease; hence the fatal dose of this toxin for man could not possibly be determined. Nor has there ever been a case of botulism reported in man, fatal or not, in which anything more than the roughest of guesses could be made as to the amount of toxin responsible. By the roughest of guesses, I mean suggestions like this one, that man must be extraordinarily susceptible to botulinus toxin, because so-and-so died after merely tasting poisoned food, without actually swallowing any. How much might one swallow when he tastes without swallowing, and how much of this might be toxin? We do not know how susceptible man is compared with the mouse, and I am confident that we shall not find out unless war comes. Of course, it is possible that human beings may be *even more* susceptible than mice; but, rather than give weight to this altogether unfounded idea, let us look at the second assumption.

This one is really buried deep under the arithmetic. The Camp Detrick mice were injected *into the belly* ("intraperitoneally"). The assumption is that either man's susceptibility to the toxin would be just the same by injection and by a more accessible route of inoculation—say, via drinking water or inhaled air—or else that some fantastically clever military device could distribute the gram or the ounce of toxin uniformly among its millions of victims by injection. Let us pass over the latter idea; it has a very low order of military practicability. As for injection versus ingestion or inhalation, we may be sure that, wherever all three routes are effective, the last two will always require much larger doses. Both the skin and the cells that line the respiratory and alimentary tracts are among our most important defenses against illness. Without them we might all succumb rapidly to infections or poisons which this surface armor keeps at bay. The process of injection at once penetrates this redoubtable outer circle of defenses and deposits the poison or infection directly in the tissues. Now, while injection can be accomplished in other ways than with the doctor's syringe and needle—with a snake's tooth, for instance, or a dagger or with a piece of shrapnel—it is distinctly not a practicable method for the dissemination of BW agents. This being true, it follows that the killing dose of botulinus toxin for man in actual BW would have to be very much higher than that indicated by mouse-man arithmetic, whether mice and men are alike in sensitivity to the poison or not.

Conditions affecting the general problem of dissemination of BW agents would still further increase the killing dose of an agent, particularly one like botulinus toxin, which does not propagate itself, since it is a poison and not an infective agent. But this is a more general factor modifying the potency of BW agents, and we shall return to it later. Let us conclude at this point that an ounce of crystalline botulinus toxin could undoubtedly kill a large number of persons, but that the number would not be so large as arithmetic alone suggests.

Having offered you a little reassurance for botulinus toxin, however, I must now, as I warned you, proceed to take it away. For when we turn from a poison like botulinus toxin —even though it be a superlative poison—to the true infective agents, we face a different kind of problem. It is not hard to show that the potency of infective agents may compare with that of poisons in general much as the killing power of the atom bomb compares, weight for weight, with that of conventional high explosives. There is no lack of evidence on this point for infection versus poisoning of animals; and here we have, in addition, some direct evidence for man—not a great deal and not nearly so precise as experimental data but enough to make the point clear.

Consider first an example for our laboratory friend, the white mouse. I have already mentioned that mice can be infected and killed, uniformly, by injecting into them a single pair of pneumococci or a single bacillus of tularemia. It would be interesting to compute the effective *weight* of such a killing dose. This can be done with sufficient accuracy by taking the pneumococcus unit (two bacteria surrounded by a capsule) as a sphere 3 microns in diameter. (A micron is $\frac{1}{1000}$ millimeter, or about $\frac{1}{25000}$ inch.) The volume of such a sphere would be about 14 cubic microns. Since the density of all living matter is very close to that of water, we may say that 1 cubic micron weighs approximately one-billionth of a milligram. It follows that 1 milligram of pneumococcal substance would contain about 700 million killing doses for the mouse, or more than twenty times as many as 1 milligram of the most potent of poisons, botulinus toxin.

This is only the beginning. Although the pneumococcus is highly infective for the mouse, it is a comparatively large germ. The bacillus of tularemia is a small one, and again a single bacillus is enough to kill a mouse. Consider a tiny cylinder, about $\frac{1}{5}$ micron in diameter and $\frac{1}{2}$ micron long. Its volume would be less than $\frac{1}{50}$ cubic micron, and its potency for the mouse on a weight basis therefore some

700 times as great as that of the pneumococcus, or about 15,000 times as great as that of botulinus toxin!

There is no reason to believe that even this order of potency represents a maximum for infection. If we could calculate the potency of some of the viruses for the mouse, we would probably find it to be as much greater than that of the tularemia bacillus as the potency of the tularemia bacillus is greater than that of the pneumococcus. But we cannot do this accurately, for we do not know the size of the infecting unit of any animal virus.

When we turn our attention to infection of man we again confront the difficulties we had with botulinus toxin in mice and men, plus some others that apply to infective agents as distinct from toxins. Toxins do not multiply in the tissues of the host. Consequently we can estimate their effects for larger or smaller hosts of a single species on the basis of host weight. The toxin must be distributed through the host to exert its effect, and hence the bigger the host, the greater will be the amount of toxin needed. But infective agents do multiply in the tissues, and the weight basis does not hold at all. As it is distributed through the body of the host, the infective agent multiplies; hence the bigger the host, the more extensive the distribution, and the greater the possible final number of germs. It takes about the same number of virulent anthrax bacilli to infect the guinea pig or the rabbit, even though the rabbit weighs about ten times as much as the guinea pig. If two species differ in sensitivity to a given infective agent it is not because of their size but because of biological differences between the species.

It is therefore quite unjustified to compute dosages of infective agents for man from animal data by the sort of weight-for-weight arithmetic we used for botulinus toxin. It is possible, indeed, that with certain germs, like those of tularemia or brucellosis, a single bacterium may be enough to infect man. This has been suggested for the plague bacillus as well, but we do not know for sure that it is true for any of them. And, moreover, since there is not a priori way of estimating with any degree of accuracy the relative susceptibility of animals and man to any given infection, we cannot hope to arrive at human dosage values along this path of reasoning. Yet we can be pretty sure of one thing: dosages of highly infective agents for man are likely to be *lower* rather than higher than would be expected on a weight basis.

If we are to learn anything of the potency of BW agents for man, we must get our information from man directly. Probably the best way to get it is from accidental infections in which the infecting dose was estimated. Of the many accidental infections of man that have been recorded, I know of two that are worth citing in which an attempt was made to estimate the infecting dose. Neither of these infections was fatal. Both were air-borne, so that the agent entered the body by inhalation; and only the second one deals with a germ that may be considered a BW agent as we have characterized it. It is nevertheless worth our while to examine both cases in some detail.

The first case concerns that most familiar of disease germs of man, the streptococcus, whose effects nearly everyone has felt at some time or other as a sore throat, a bronchopneumonia, a scarlet fever, or an even more serious case of blood poisoning. The accidental infection occurred as a severe sore throat in a researcher who had been working with a team studying the distribution of this germ through the air of Army hospital wards. Since the length of time she had been exposed and the number of streptococci in the air she breathed were both known, it was possible to estimate that the dose she received by inhalation was not more than 1,280 streptococci. You will recall that the streptococcus is a chain of spherical germs. Let us say that each of these 1,280 streptococci was a chain of four cocci, each of which was roughly a sphere about 0.8 micron in diameter. By the sort of reasoning we used before we find that 1 gram of these germs would then contain enough to produce sore throats in about 700 million human beings! If we overlook the fact that this was an infecting dose rather than a killing one and that the number is based on a single case, we find the streptococcus to be roughly one hundred times as potent, gram for gram, as crystalline botulinus toxin. And be it noted that our arithmetic is much less doubtful for the streptococcus, for we are dealing with man directly and with a route of infection (inhalation) that we have come to regard as eminently suitable for BW.

Yet the streptococcus would not be considered suitable for BW, mainly because its infectivity seems to be very variable. Many of us carry large numbers of these germs in the nose, mouth, and throat without being ill, although when we expel them by coughing or sneezing we may infect others with them. Perhaps the particular streptococcus that we have just been talking about was more infective than most or this particular victim of it may have been abnormally susceptible to it. We could not tell without data for large numbers of similar cases, and these we do not have. It is nevertheless revealing to discover that this rather common disease germ can be much more potent in causing disease than the most potent of poisons.

The second case of accidental infection in which the infecting dose for man was estimated was caused by a characteristic potential BW agent, psittacosis virus, and, in fact, occurred in a laboratory worker at Camp Detrick. The subject had handled an ampule containing a concentrated suspension of this virus and became aware only while doing so that the ampule leaked and was spraying a fine jet of the virus-containing fluid against the palm of his hand. He made a record of the event, preserved the ampule after having it sterilized, and then forgot the whole matter in the rush of work until twelve days later, when he found himself ill with psittacosis. Having recovered, he and his colleagues undertook to reconstruct the incident so as to measure the infecting dose. They knew that this virus does not infect man through the skin, but probably only by inhalation. Using the original ampule, which was found to have a tiny hole in its base, they therefore sprayed a harmless bacterium against a man's hand just as the virus had been sprayed originally and measured the concentration of the bacterium raised by this procedure as a cloud in the air at the level of the man's nose and mouth. Knowing the concentration of virus in the batch of ampules from which the original one had been taken it was a simple matter to estimate the amount of virus that had been inhaled. The amount appeared in two trials to be, respectively, 39 and 97 virus units, the unit being the dose required to kill 50 per cent of a group of mice which had been injected with virus into the brain.

It would be illuminating to apply to this figure the sort of arithmetic we have used for bacteria, but unfortunately we do not know the size of the psittacosis-virus unit. What we do know is that there were a billion and a half virus units for the mouse in each cubic centimeter of the fluid in the ampule. One cubic centimeter weighs about 1 gram. Since the infecting dose for man had been estimated to be not more than 100 mouse units, it follows that each cubic centimeter of the preparation contained enough virus to infect at least 15 million human beings. This represents again a potency higher than that obtained for crystalline botulinus toxin by doubtful arithmetic. But let us take note that here as with the streptococcus, except that the dosage is based on but one instance, we are dealing with human infection directly and with the route of inoculation that seems most practicable in BW—inhalation. And what seems most striking is that this was not a purified preparation but a routine virus soup, in which the virus proper comprised only a very small fraction of the total dissolved and suspended matter. The preparation was a ground-up suspension of yolk sacs from fertile eggs in which the virus had been grown, the yolk sacs having been mixed with ten times their weight of broth.

If all our previous potency values have had an element of the theoretical about them, this one seems staggeringly practical. It is hard to make crystalline botulinus toxin, and it might well be more feasible to use an unpurified and very much less potent bacterial broth if the toxin were to be disseminated in warfare. We cannot easily, if at all, prepare bacteria free from all extraneous material and disseminate them by the gram. But here is a run-of-the-laboratory suspension of psittacosis virus, easily made in small laboratories in, say, quart lots, which appears to be at least twice as effective in producing disability in man, gram for gram, as the pure toxin crystals. A quart of such a psittacosis-virus preparation, if you feel the need of one last figure, would contain, according to our computation, enough virus to infect more than 7 billion human beings, or about three times the total population of the earth.

Add the fact that psittacosis is a self-propagating disease. Naturally occurring outbreaks have all been small, perhaps in part because each started from a single case, or because they occurred within the confines of laboratories. If BW were to induce a high concentration of initial cases, severe epidemicity might result.

But let us end this chapter on a qualifying note. It is one thing to say that a gram, an ounce, or a quart of any given agent *contains enough* germs to infect so many men. To bring about such an event in practice is a horse of an entirely different color. Here we face the problem of the dissemination of BW agents. Let it be clearly understood for the present that there is no conceivable way in which any particular weight or volume of any agent could be spread over more than a very limited area of the earth. Just how large this area could be is a matter of mechanics, engineering, and meteorology. It would depend on the kind and size of the disseminating device, on the number of such devices and the manner in which they were set in action, and on wind, weather, and other conditions. But the target area would necessarily be limited, and accordingly the actual effect—without allowing for epidemicity—would always be less than the theoretical potency. For the moment let us recognize only that BW agents could be potent enough and to spare.

8. PRODUCTION

IF we have come safely through the perilous arithmetic of the last chapter we know that BW agents can pack a mighty wallop in a tiny bundle. They are so powerful that we need scarcely think of them in units larger than grams or ounces. It is hard to imagine that more than this would be needed for any military job. But, you may say, radium and plutonium are potent, too. Yet these things are so rare, so hard to make, and therefore so extravagantly expensive that one doesn't talk of grams or ounces of them quite so flippantly as one does, say, of aspirin—or even of silver or gold. Are BW agents rare and precious? I have already suggested that pure crystalline botulinus toxin or bacteria naked and alone are indeed rare, probaby too rare for any practical purpose; but that psittacosis virus, in a surpassingly powerful soup, could easily be made in quart lots. It is time now to look into this whole question more particularly. How would BW agents be made, and how difficult would it be to make them?

We know that the agents themselves are almost universally available. They are present wherever there is infection and wherever men in white coats ply the profession of science in the little back rooms of hospitals, medical schools, public-health institutes, veterinary stations, and greenhouses. Both the native bugs and the foreign ones and the men and things needed to handle them will be found in laboratories from

America to Russia, from China to Uruguay, from Puerto Rico to Java, from South Africa to Sweden—in every reasonably well-developed country on earth and in some undeveloped ones. If the bug is not at hand, a letter will bring enough of it to start production. The initial cost is a postage stamp—or nothing at all.

The first production problem is to plant and cultivate and harvest the crop. These homely farming words are used not merely by analogy; they are apt. The production of germs is much like raising corn. In proper soil, suitably tended, both grow from small to large, from few to many. The differences are in the kind of soil and the manner of tending.

The production of BW agents is in the first place a work of cultivation. Its materials are the initial germs (the seed) and a suitable culture medium (the soil). But growing germs is more like greenhouse or even apartment-house gardening than like farming in the open; the germ crops are raised in pots—in test tubes, bottles, trays, tanks, or vats. These are placed or arranged so that the growth temperature is right and so that the growing germs, depending on their particular needs, have either plenty of air or a restricted amount or no air at all. Some prefer to be left undisturbed; others do better when shaken or when air is forced through the medium or even when the medium is continuously circulated and changed.

The germs are first grown in small lots on a laboratory scale. These lots may be used as seed cultures, and at this level or at the next one—on the pilot-plant scale—the kind of soil and the kind of tending needed for each germ are determined. Then, if necessary, mass-production methods can be developed on engineering principles that are well established in the brewing and other fermentation industries and in large vaccine laboratories. Before such mass production or even pilot-plant production is instituted, however, each kind of germ must be studied and "developed" at the laboratory-scale level to determine its suitability for BW and particularly to check on or improve its stability under the conditions for which it is intended.

Production problems, then, up to the point of harvest, will be largely matters of the availability, procurement, and cost—first, of raw materials; secondly, of laboratory and plant equipment; and, thirdly, of personnel and know-how.

Raw materials, for the most part, are as widely available as the germs themselves. For the agents of human and animal diseases they are usually the tissues or products of animals. For bacteria in seed lots meat broth is the customary basic medium, enriched for germs that need enrichment with sugar, blood, or other animal fluids, or with such vitamin-rich foods as yeast or liver extracts. For the rickettsiae and viruses whole tissue in the living state must be used; and here the developing chick embryo provides a nearly universal medium.

So long as small-scale operations are involved such foods present no great problem of procurement or cost. The provision of fertile eggs on a large scale for the germs that need them may have no practical alternative but is unlikely to require one. Virus research demands large numbers of eggs anyway; and the number needed for BW production is not likely to be much if any greater than that needed for more routine purposes, like measurements of potency. The number of eggs required for the production of standard yellow-fever vaccine probably runs to several thousand per day to meet ordinary needs. BW virus production would be a very similar undertaking. The problem tends to be simplified for the rickettsiae and the viruses by the facts, first, that it is usually practicable to obtain high concentrations of the agent in the fluids or tissues of the developing egg and, secondly, that the infectivity of these agents is likely to be high, so that, as with psittacosis virus, the final volumes needed for any military purpose would be comparatively small and well within reach.

For the bacteria similar considerations might apply if there were no alternative to the use of meat, animal fluids, and other materials that must also serve as food for men and animals. In wartime particularly, meat becomes a strategic product, and the diversion of manpower and machines from the productive work of peace to the nonproductive work of war inevitably aggravates shortages. Given a sufficiently high priority, BW production would if necessary merely increase the unavoidable dislocations of war. But the experiences of World War II, both in BW development and in the practice of bacteriological laboratories elsewhere, showed that diversion of strategic food materials can be largely avoided. Bacteria can be grown very well on substitute foods, some of them industrial products that might otherwise be wasted. Such substitutes have included soy-bean extracts, a cheap by-product of the milk industry called "pepticase," and corn-steep liquor, a waste product rich in vitamins. For growing fungi that produce disease in plants, peanut hulls, tomato waste, and similar food sources have been found useful.

It seems fair to say that neither the procurement nor the cost of the raw materials for BW production would pose serious problems. The standard materials are widely available and, from the military viewpoint, cheap; and many of these could if necessary be replaced by still cheaper materials.

There would also be needed relatively large numbers of living animals and plants for developmental research and for potency testing during the course of production. These experimental hosts would in turn require feeding and tending, and this would add appreciably to costs of production. But even if the potency of BW agents were only a tiny fraction of what it is, there would be nothing in the whole production picture to compare with the cost of mining and purifying fissionable uranium or of producing plutonium.

Other production problems in BW are even less serious. The laboratory and plant equipment needed are entirely similar to those used all over the world for peacetime bacteriological work except for the special requirement of safety. The existing equipment of breweries, fermentation factories, penicillin-production plants, and vaccine laboratories could be converted to BW with few changes; or the principles used in their construction could be applied with little modification to the construction of BW installations.

The same applies to personnel and know-how. Wherever there are medical and veterinary schools and plant-science laboratories there are scientists capable of undertaking BW research, development, and production. The methods required are either matters of common knowledge and standard practice throughout the world, or else they are easily derived from principles that are universally understood. There are likely to be many ways of doing any particular job rather than just one. If we have developed some good ones that we are keeping secret, it is entirely probable that scientists and engineers in other lands, starting from scratch, may develop others that are equally good if not better.

Let us look at a few examples bearing on production problems of potential BW agents, taken from technical reports of the work done at Camp Detrick. In one paper is a report on methods for production of botulinus toxin. The end product here was a crude soup rather than the pure crystals of toxin. In fact, it was by this method that Dr. Lamanna obtained the large amounts of toxic broth needed for preparation of the crystals. The crude soup would probably be more practicable for offensive BW than the crystals but would be needed in large amounts, since its average potency was only about 30 million fatal mouse doses to the ounce. In this work it was found that practical liquid mediums could be made of "readily available and relatively inexpensive ingredients," including cheap grades of casein and glucose and the waste product, corn-steep liquor.

Another paper describes a medium made from an infusion of potatoes and containing glycerin but having no meat or meat products, which was "equal in every respect" to the more common meat medium for growing the bacteria of glanders or melioidosis.

Among several reports giving technical details applicable to the production of the highly virulent swine strain of *Brucella* is one that describes a continuous flow system on a small-laboratory scale, capable of producing about a pint of fluid every 8 hours and of being "operated safely . . . for prolonged periods of time with little manual attention." Each pint contained *Brucella* germs in an amount expressed by a number just under 2 followed by 13 zeros, or 20 trillion. This, I repeat, is a laboratory-scale system. Another report on the same microbe notes that as many as 800 billion germs per gram could be produced in 60-gram lots with "standard equipment . . . readily available in most laboratories."

Experiments with the fungus that causes San Joaquin Valley fever, *Coccidioides immitis*, showed that more than a trillion germs per ounce could be produced in a simple fluid medium containing only glucose and certain salts. This concentration could be increased more than threefold by the addition to the medium of minute amounts of crude lecithin, a fatlike substance containing phosphorus, obtained from egg yolk and many animal tissues. In the lecithin-containing medium the fungus was infective for guinea pigs by inhalation with an infecting dose of not more than 1,350 fungus particles or spores, which means that the culture contained more than 4 billion guinea-pig doses per ounce. This high concentration could be increased another 50 per cent by growing the fungus in a medium containing meat products and glucose.

From these examples we may safely generalize that the production of BW agents poses no insuperable problems. If the agent is at hand and a method of growing it is available, the method can be improved to increase the yield, and means for large-scale production can be devised if they are needed. Where relatively scarce or expensive ingredients have been used for test-tube cultures, more abundant and cheaper products can usually be substituted for larger scale lots. Each germ is likely to be a separate problem that must be developed separately; but such development need not be expected to require anything very special in the way of material, equipment, or skill.

The end product of this first phase of production for BW is a harvest of germs in laboratory or production-plant containers: flasks, bottles, carboys, drums, or comparable vessels. To transform these products into usable BW weapons, they must be emptied into containers of a different sort, which are to be used for dissemination of the agent in warfare. These could possibly be simple vials, ampules, or flasks; but they are more likely to be specially constructed devices which incorporate a disseminating mechanism of some kind—in other words, BW munitions. This much is obvious as a matter of principle; but no details of any modern development of this sort have been published. They are part of the secret know-how of BW. Yet the general requirements are not hidden. If an understanding of the properties of infective agents is combined with a mechanical skill and ingenuity which need be neither extraordinary nor scarce, there will surely be an effective answer, and probably more than one, to every question that arises.

One of the larger questions is that of maintaining the agent alive and active during periods of transportation and storage under field conditions. This is part of the problem of the stabilization of BW agents. Several principles and methods that have been devised in recent years to meet normal laboratory and plant requirements might be made use of for BW. Some of the most delicate germs, like the spirochetes, can be preserved alive and virulent for several years by freezing them in dry ice. Many others can be kept alive for long periods by drying them rapidly from the frozen state and then merely storing them in sealed containers in a cool place. Ordinary refrigeration alone or rapid drying alone may be sufficient in some instances. Any of these methods is likely to be more successful if the agent is first prepared or suspended in a medium that protects it against damage, probably by covering each germ with a protective layer. Protective media may differ with individual agents, and it may therefore be necessary to find out about them by tests on the individual kind of germ.

In the production process from beginning to end and in fact in every phase of research and development with highly infective agents things must be done to protect the working personnel against infection and to prevent leakage of the agent into the environment. This problem of safety is not peculiar to BW, but for the most part it is sure to be more serious in BW work than elsewhere. Wherever agents of human disease are handled the handlers must be protected; and wherever any disease agent is dealt with susceptible hosts, whether animal or plant, must be shielded from accidental infection. In normal peacetime practice such problems are not usually difficult to cope with, and well-developed standard practices are sufficient to meet ordinary needs. Occasional accidents are often due to carelessness, an incompletely avoidable human failing.

Outside of BW the most serious hazards have been met in fieldwork with such diseases as yellow fever or typhus or with serious epidemic diseases in areas where the researcher has entered with no more protection than that of the population he was trying to aid. Research with highly infective agents in public-health laboratories has brought its toll of accidental infections. Until recently all the standard procedures for protection of the worker did little to prevent such infections. But experience gained from these accidents and in particular during the course of work with highly infective agents at Camp Detrick has shown that safety is realizable within small limits of error. The most dangerous agents to man and probably also to other hosts are those capable of being air-borne. As soon as the subject of air-borne infection itself had reached the point where we could appreciate this fact, it became possible to devise adequate means for protection against it. Some of the details of one investigation in which the problem was met and solved will be given in the next chapter. This particular solution, which is not necessarily the only possible one, involved, first, means for handling the germs in a completely closed system, so that the operators never came in contact with them; secondly, the air from the system was literally burned—by passing it through an incinerator—before it was released into the outside environment.

Air incineration, as an example of the special safety precautions required in a BW installation, calls for equipment different from that found in most peacetime laboratories or plants devoted to bacteriological work. It represents, as do the more stringent requirements for safety in general, an adaptation that might have to be made to convert normal installations to the ends of BW. The conversion would not be difficult and would not require either materials or skills other than those universally available wherever the two fields of engineering and bacteriology are well developed.

A story is told about the successful operation of one safety precaution at Camp Detrick which I can embellish from knowledge that was common to the inhabitants of the neighboring city of Frederick during the war. Mr. Merck tells it this way in his Westinghouse Forum address:

"The doubts of the health authorities of the municipality in which the main biological warfare experimental station was located were aroused—probably by the size of the establishment—regarding the adequacy of the sanitary measures. The local health officer determined to test the sewage of the establishment where it entered the city system. Imagine his surprise when confronted with the baffling fact that his tests showed the sewage sterile—perhaps the only sterile sewage in the world. Had he tested the ventilating outlet flues from the laboratories and the pilot-plant operations, he would have found them sterile too."

Sterile sewage! Camp Detrick had two kinds of sewage, the "classified" kind and the "unclassified" or ordinary kind. It is evident that both were sterilized. Such a sterilizing operation might be done with steam under pressure, and would require large tanks. It may be noted that at one corner of the camp an impressive row of tanks, some as big as freight cars, some smaller, invited the gaze of the uninformed passer-by. At night a searchlight from the corner guard tower played on them and revealed the adjacent plant buildings, all visible through the cyclone fence. The view was such as to excite curiosity, and the Frederick citizenry who passed by were known to speculate on the contents of the tanks. Of the ideas that became current, the one I like best is implied in a native's wistful remark that "if I only had what was in one of those tanks I could retire for life!"

9. OFFENSE

We know how the agents of BW can be picked out, and we recognize and respect their power. We have found ways to make heaps of them, and we know they can be packed neatly into some vague sorts of bombs and stored safely away. What now? Perhaps all this has already been done down Maryland way; the newspapers do not say, nor do the technical journals. Maybe it has been done in a dozen other countries around this vexed and turbulent planet. If it has not been done today, it may be done tomorrow or the next day. We would be fools to assume otherwise, for what I have written is not secret and will not be new to those who feel the need to know it. BW bombs are cheap and easy weapons. To poor countries, if not to all others, they look like good substitutes for atomic bombs, which are strictly for the rich. In a dozen countries the military men may be saying, "Let us pile up these cheap and easy bombs; there's a storm brewing, and they may come in handy when it breaks."

But between BW bombs in refrigerated dumps and germs loosed to kill men, animals, and plants a great hiatus stretches. What, really, can these germ bombs do? And how does one get them to do it?

There is only one true way of answering this question at the moment—nobody really knows. In its modern form BW has never been used in a military operation. Until it has been used we will have no way of knowing exactly what it can do, how effective it can be, to what degree it might contribute toward victory or defeat in a World War III. This book is dedicated toward realization of the hope that we shall never know. But if we are not to know for sure, we had better guess.

We can make some pretty shrewd guesses. It would be possible to make even shrewder guesses if we had access to information that has not been made public. The Merck Report speaks of the establishment of special "field-testing" facilities for BW in Mississippi and in Utah. Field tests can be conducted so as to provide information on the manner of use and the effectiveness of BW directed against animals or plants. The experimental attacks may be made on small laboratory animals or on the species of either animal or plant intended as the real victim. The tests, moreover, can bring out facts about the effectiveness of disseminating devices, about dispersion of the agent under different weather conditions, and about its persistence and its transport by air or other vehicles. Knowing these things, one can undertake to predict what will happen in war. This is the best way, before the actual shooting starts, to match the agent to the military job, to perfect the bomb, and to determine the conditions best suited for its use. For BW directed against animals or plants a lot of the guesswork is eliminated. Where man is to be the target the guesses still loom large, but this is the kind of information upon which the use of any new weapon must be based.

Actual combat conditions may cancel all predictions and enforce a complete retooling of the machinery of war, including BW. We can paint lurid pictures of what we think World War III will be like, but nobody really knows. Even the military, steeped as it is in tradition, must recognize by now that we cannot predict the combat conditions of World War III merely by calculating from Wars I and II. In World

War I the troops in Europe suffered a very high proportion of head injuries—born out of trench warfare by perilous human curiosity. In World War II head injuries were no more common than other kinds, because there were no trenches. About the only thing we can feel reasonably sure of as to the character of a World War III is that it will probably be very different from any previous war and certainly much worse. BW may help to make it so; but its nature apart from BW may enforce drastic renovation of any predictions or plans made now, even with the help of all the knowledge available to the military but not to us. So the military, even with its inside information, must guess too; and we might as well do the same.

Let us begin by postulating, not an abstract or generalized World War III, but the war that seems at the moment most probable, in which the United States and Russia would be the principal antagonists. In such a war, whether it came within the next few years, or increasingly if it happened five, ten, or fifteen years from now, the conditions might be expected to favor BW and to favor the widest use of its resources. From a saboteur's use of botulinus toxin to contaminate the food in an airplane-factory lunchroom to a world-wide pandemic of pneumonic plague, almost anything would be possible. The most desperate measures, like the use of agents with high epidemic capacity, might be resorted to at some stage of such a conflict. For in an American-Soviet war both the physical and the ideological factors might be expected to minimize all restraints and to lend to the idea of totality in war a new and more comprehensive meaning.

The ideological aspects can be overemphasized, but they might still poison the last lingering vestige—if there were one—of war as a game played according to rules. The physical conditions would themselves encourage the use of BW in all its varied forms by either or both sides—the great land masses of the two principal combatants, insulated from one another by oceans and for the most part by intervening land; the dependence of both countries for their war potential on industrial population centers, many of them far inland; the presence in both countries of congested slum areas or equivalent breeding places of natural epidemic disease; and the relative self-sufficiency of both countries in food resources.

In such a war it seems to me naïve to suggest that BW would not be used because of the possibility that some of its agents might backfire on the user. What we have called "retroactivity" might restrain a small country from using the more highly epidemic agents in a war against an immediate neighbor; but the fact is that large-scale BW, like the atomic bomb, is not adapted to such wars anyway. Smaller scale BW offensives or sabotage or BW limited to agents of low self-propagating capacity might be used in any war. But BW on the grand scale calls for war on the grand scale—the intercontinental war that an American-Russian conflict presupposes. We could not hope to devastate Soviet territory without injuring ourselves no matter how we did it; nor could the Russians hope to damage us without hurting themselves. Retroactivity at worst would be one of the calculated risks of the new total war, like radioactive dusts returning from our own atomic bombs at the antipodes.

Primarily BW would be directed against civilians rather than against military populations. Because its effects would be delayed and because of the chances of backfiring aggravated by propinquity, BW would probably not be used in battles in which the opposing forces were in close contact or in rapid or alternating movement. If effective vaccination and other assured defenses were available to the attacking force and particularly if they were thought not to be available to the defender, even such uses might become feasible; but on the whole the active battleground looks like the least favorable terrain for BW, and infantry in action might have the least to fear from it. This would be much less true for more static military targets like army camps and training centers or for cities under siege, where BW might well be tried, its tactics governed largely by the incubation period of agents and their potential retroactivity. But it is the industrial civilian areas that would be most liable to BW attacks and particularly those from which vital military supplies were flowing, situated well within enemy territory, so that they would be insulated against retroactivity.

In such areas the target might be man directly or it might be his food supply or his sources of other essentials derived from animals or plants. Or these latter might be attacked more directly for a broader purpose than to knock out a single industrial center. Within the limits of this strategic objective nearly all the resources of BW would find a place, intended to destroy animal or plant life or make it unfit for human use or to kill or incapacitate human beings or to demoralize them. Relative emphasis on physical or psychological effects, on rapid destruction or an insidious sort of creeping paralysis, the attempt at a single finishing blow or at a succession of nuisance attacks—all these variations would be governed by the immediate objective in its military context, whether the attack were made in confidence or desperation, at the brave outset or toward the bitter end of the war. The range of possibilities seems to me too wide to justify particular examples.

A more restricted sort of target that would permit even greater freedom in the choice of agents and methods of BW would be an isolated military stronghold or strategic spot, like an island naval or air base. Such a place might be neutralized by BW, particularly if there were no need to capture or occupy it; for here the possibility of backfiring could be virtually eliminated and the most highly retroactive agents used with relative impunity. A single small plane ought to be able to carry a sufficient BW bomb load to make an island of several hundred square miles uninhabitable for many months or longer.

Think back on the potency of BW agents. Consider their capacity to cause damage or death in man, animals, or plants, in individuals or in populations. Think of the way some of them can be self-propagating. Put these ideas together with twenty or more distinct BW agents, to be used separately or in combinations with one another or with chemical agents. Then think of the different ways in which each agent or combination might be used in war. This is the foundation for a guess as to what offensive BW might do. Then, if your imagination will carry you far enough, think of the possible combinations of BW with other forms of warfare, old and new, with BW coming before, along with, or after the others. The result, if you can picture it, is the new total war.

But all of this does not tell us *how* BW could be made to do these things. How would BW agents be spread? And how sure could their spreaders be that the germs would find their hosts and have the expected effects on them? These are crucial questions, with no real answers possible short of actual trials in war but with enough known to allow us to make guesses that ought to serve.

Methods of spreading antiplant agents of the chemical type, like 2,4-D, have been proved by extensive practice and are no problem. Their use for killing weeds, along with the related process of disseminating DDT for the destruction of insects, has become a flourishing industry and can be handled successfully on both small and large scales. There is a "fog generator" on the market, designed for these products, which is capable of spraying very extensive areas—according to the manufacturer's leaflet, "farms, ranches, estates . . . fields and forests . . . cities, villages." In the interval after a lecture I once gave, a representative of a company that makes such instruments handed me a circular describing them. I had been talking to a group of engineers on BW and had ended my talk with a plea for the prevention of war. The gentleman in question, however, apparently mistaking my purpose and with the air of an inveterate salesman, hinted that his generator might be useful for the dissemination of BW agents and left the circular with me as an advertisement!

No, there is no particular problem about spreading chemical agents, including 2,4-D; but the dissemination of true agents of BW is less simple. The agents of infection cannot be dissolved like chemicals without destroying them; they cannot withstand even moderately high temperatures; and any kind of rough handling, like spraying them through high-pressure nozzles, is likely to do them injury. Yet the problem of getting them from bomb to target, once their peculiar properties are understood, is not fundamentally different from that of spreading chemical agents, and I have no doubt that human ingenuity can manage it if it has not already found ways to do so. I have great confidence in the skill of engineers.

We can divide the dissemination problem for true BW agents into two parts, one of which might be marked "miscellaneous," and the other, "large-scale air-borne offense." It is the second one that is the problem, but let us take them in order.

In the first, or wastebasket, category fall all the means of spreading BW agents that would use routes of infection other than the inhaled air. We may add small-scale air-borne attacks, like pollution of the ingoing air of an air-conditioned theater. This last would be an act of sabotage, and the germs might conceivably be introduced with a *Flit* gun. The deposition of infected vectors (insects and the like) or of diseased animals, both being intended to infect man, would probably require hardly more elaborate equipment. The deliberate pollution of food for human use and any possible attempts at contact infection, directly, indirectly, or through contaminated weapons, would also be limited in purpose and would fall largely within the bailiwick of the saboteur. Such attempts might work. They would require nothing extraordinary in the way of apparatus; ingenious gadgets could be devised to make them easier or to disguise their purpose so as to protect the saboteur. Their results might be sufficient to give them military value, but they would not be among the major effects of BW. If the importance of BW as a whole rested on such methods there would be little reason for this book.

In fact these restricted offensive means characterize the primitive BW of the past and contrast sharply with the potentialities of modern germ warfare. All BW attacks that are known or thought to have been made in wars up to and including World War II fall into this category. The results for the most part were trivial. In two instances, neither of which is completely authenticated, they seem to have been more serious; but even if they were BW attacks their success can be attributed to chance, and it is doubtful if they could have been repeated.

Most of the instances in the historical record of actual BW show no great success. Pasteur, for instance, was the first to try destroying animal pests with induced infection, inspired by his work with a germ he had found to be highly infective for rabbits, the fowl-cholera bacillus. In 1887 he sent his young assistant Dr. Loir to Rheims to destroy rabbits in an enclosure above the wine cellars of a Madame Pommery. It seems that the rabbits, burrowing above the cellar, loosened stones that fell on Madame Pommery's champagne bottles; and Pasteur, staunch ally of the French wine industry, undertook to help. Dr. Loir infected some of the rabbits with the fowl-cholera germ. Three days later thirty-two rabbit cadavers were found; and the rest of the rabbits, if there were any, were frightened off. Encouraged by this success, Pasteur sent Loir to Sydney the following year to destroy the rabbits that were then causing serious damage in Australia. This second attempt was less successful. The rabbit disease did not spread, and the Australian cattle breeders, scared by the possibility of danger to their herds, campaigned against the Pasteur process so that it was Loir rather than the rabbits who retreated.

Thereafter repeated attempts were made to destroy rats with the bacillus of mouse typhoid; but the results were variable. Rats that were infected but did not die developed a solid immunity and could not be killed in subsequent attempts. Similarly unsuccessful efforts were made to kill insect pests with germs infective for them, instigated by such famous bacteriologists as Metchnikoff, the discoverer of the germ-eating cells of the body, the phagocytes, and d'Herelle, codiscoverer of viruses that infect bacteria, the bacteriophages. One Frenchman is said to have worked on the problem of germ warfare against insects for twenty years and then to have abandoned it, but in the persistent belief that it could be solved. This chapter of primitive BW is evidently closed now, having been replaced by highly successful modern methods of killing both rats and insects with chemical rather than biological agents, like 1080 and ANTU for rats and DDT for insects.

Well-authenticated attempts at BW by the Germans in World War I seem also to have had no very remarkable effects. The Merck Report notes that "there is incontrovertible evidence . . . that in 1915 German agents inoculated horses and cattle leaving United States ports for shipment to the Allies with disease-producing bacteria." Similar attempts, using glanders against horses and anthrax against cattle, are known to have been made or planned in Bucharest in 1916; and it has been alleged that another attempt, possibly successful, was made in France in 1917. There are also some ambiguous reports that German agents in Zurich during World War I tried, with possibly some degree of success, to spread cholera among the human population of surrounding countries, notably Italy; and in World War II the Germans are said to have used Russian prisoners of war for experiments in BW. But the record treats these matters, at worst, as outrages against decency rather than as military successes.

In 1934 the British journalist Wickham Steed described secret German documents reportedly in his possession which gave details of experiments, both completed and proposed, for air-borne BW attacks. Some of Steed's details have a modern and convincing ring—for example, his report of field tests in which a harmless bacillus was sprayed in several stations of the Paris *métro* and its dissemination measured by recovery cultures. Some of these tests are said to have failed and others to have been highly successful. Quoted excerpts of the documents indicate the purpose of the experiments to have been "the infection of large cities like Paris or London" by contamination of their underground railways. Steed's allegations were vigorously denied by Ernst Burkhardt of the *Hamburger Tageblatt,* who suggested that the documents were either forgeries or else related to experiments on the measurement of air currents for a nonmilitary purpose like town planning. Although Steed continued to insist on their authenticity and on the validity of his interpretation, no public confirmation of either has ever appeared, nor are the experiments, if they were in fact conducted, known to have been translated into actual BW attacks.

Of the two instances of alleged BW with more serious consequences, one goes back to the eighteenth century or earlier;

the other has to do with the spreading of bubonic plague in China by the Japanese in 1940.

The early instance was mentioned by a French writer on BW in 1939 and again, in different form and perhaps relating to a quite different event, by Dr. Selman A. Waksman at *America's Town Meeting of the Air* on May 16, 1946. In the first reference, the statement is attributed to the noted French bacteriologist Charles Nicolle that in 1763 the English General Amherst, governor of Nova Scotia, and his subordinate Colonel Bouquet, wanted to try to spread smallpox among the native tribes of Canada by means of contaminated clothing. It is not indicated that this was actually done or, if it was, that there were any serious results. Dr. Waksman, the discoverer of streptomycin, made the following remark without additional details: "The troops of the terrifying Spanish conqueror Pizarro are said to have presented the Indians with clothes from smallpox-infected patients, resulting in the death of 3 million Indians." If this is true * it may have been the most extravagant mass murder in all history. Yet even if true it is the sort of event that could happen only if a new disease of high epidemicity were introduced, under condi-

---

* Since writing the above I have found an authoritative little book (Stearn, E. W. and Stearn, A. E., *The Effect of Smallpox on the Destiny of the Amerindian*, Bruce Humphries, Inc., Boston, 1945) in which Amherst and Bouquet are clearly implicated as having used BW against Indians, and which throws light on Waksman's statement. The writers cite extant documentary evidence which shows that, following a pointed suggestion by Amherst in 1763, Capt. Ecuyer of Bouquet's command at Fort Pitt transmitted two blankets and a handkerchief from the smallpox hospital to two Indian chiefs. A serious outbreak of smallpox subsequently appeared among the tribes of the Ohio. As for the three million Indians, however, there seems to be no evidence of malicious intent. Stearn and Stearn note that "Sir Harry Johnston estimates that between the years 1550 and 1850 at least three million Amerindians died from smallpox in the West Indies, Central and South America." The disease seems to have been introduced into America by the expeditions of Columbus and Cortez, but not intentionally. It is interesting that syphilis, which appeared in Europe in the closing years of the fifteenth century under the guise of a new disease, is thought to have been brought back by Columbus's sailors, who may thus have exchanged smallpox for syphilis.

tions favoring its spread, into a population that had neither immunity against it nor any knowledge of modern science. It may have happened, but it is not the kind of result that present-day strategists could count on.

As for Japanese BW attacks on China, the record is confused but very suggestive. Mr. Merck, in 1946, went so far as to say that "there is no evidence that the enemy [in the context, clearly Japan] ever resorted to this means of warfare [BW]." Yet there are rather well documented if incompletely proved accounts of repeated attacks by Japanese planes, one or a few at a time, in which rice grains, wisps of cotton rags, and other materials, presumably contaminated with plague bacilli, were dropped in areas of central China where plague had never been known to occur since medical records have been kept. There is no doubt that plague broke out in these areas, that one hundred and fifty or more cases of plague occurred at the time, nearly all of them fatal, and that the disease has persisted in these and adjoining regions of China down to the present. The attacks themselves, moreover, seem to have been well authenticated by observers on the spot. The conclusion that BW was involved was evidently accepted not only by Chinese public-health authorities but also by Harrison Forman, *New York Times* correspondent, and by Dr. Thomas Parran, then Surgeon-General of the United States Public Health Service. Furthermore the Merck Report makes it plain that the Japanese were in fact working intensively on BW from 1936 until as late as 1945.

These circumstances might be sufficiently incriminating were it not for two others. Plague has existed, probably for many centuries, in more southern areas of China than those involved in these incidents, and it might have spread north without Japanese intervention. Of more direct significance, plague bacilli were never isolated from the materials dropped by the Japanese planes, although several attempts to do so seem to have been made. Success in this undertaking would have clinched the matter. Failure may well have been due to inadequate laboratory facilities on the spot and to excessive delay in making the tests; plague bacilli cannot stay alive in the environment indefinitely. These negative findings are therefore not conclusive, but they leave the allegation of BW incompletely proved.

Even if we accept the conclusion that these incidents represented true offensive BW, we cannot consider the method used as anything but very primitive, or, as we called it in the 1942 Report, "amateurish." If it was BW, it is plain that the Japanese themselves must have found the results unworthy of extensive repetition, for they do not seem to have tried again during five additional years of war. Like the incident suggested by Dr. Waksman, this kind of attack could have succeeded only under very special circumstances: where plague was absent although all the conditions for its spread were present, including an abundance of rats or other susceptible rodents and a crowded, poverty-stricken human population without adequate public-health facilities or other applications of modern medical knowledge. It is not a testimonial to the effectiveness of present-day BW.

Returning from this historical digression to our wastebasket category of offensive means of BW we find a few other methods, some of which might have considerable military importance. These are attempts to contaminate reservoirs used for drinking water and nearly if not quite all means of attack on animals and growing plants, including the contamination of animal pasturage or feeds and the infection of vegetation from the air. To some degree these latter methods would overlap with large-scale attacks on man via the air-borne route of infection. Otherwise, although they might be devastatingly successful, they would probably not require any very elaborate equipment. The pollution of a reservoir might not call for anything more than dropping into it a sufficient quantity of the agent, say in liquid form, in any simple container that could be depended upon to discharge its contents into the water. Mixing would be accomplished by diffusion and by the movements of the water. Stabilization of the agent, so that it would withstand the effects of suspension in water and of sunlight for the necessary periods of time, would have been accomplished by previous experiment. This much would probably be easy enough; the difficulty here would not be in disseminating the agent but in getting it unharmed past the filtration, chlorination, or other sanitary safeguards used to make the water fit to drink. I have mentioned before that this obstacle, combined with the uncertain infectivity of many water-borne agents, like the germs of cholera or typhoid fever, might prevent the use of such agents in BW. These problems, however, are not necessarily insoluble; and the method might be tried with other agents, like botulinus toxin.

As for attacks on animals or true BW attacks on plants (as opposed to those using 2,4-D and like chemicals), equipment that is simple and readily available could probably be used with few if any modifications. The fungi that seem most important among BW agents of plants are generally more resistant than most infective agents of man and animals and could stand rougher treatment. For animals, rapidly self-propagating agents like the viruses of rinderpest or hoof-and-mouth disease or the bacilli of Bang's disease could probably be prepared in sufficiently stable form, perhaps incorporated in feeds, and would need only to be dropped on pastures from the air. It would not be necessary to infect very large numbers of animals simultaneously in any given enclosure, for once started any of these diseases could be expected to spread rapidly through the herd. What makes the pollution of reservoirs for attacks on man difficult here makes attacks on animals easy—the sanitary safeguards are lacking. It is probably for reasons of this kind, as we have seen, that under natural conditions brucellosis (Bang's disease) spreads uncontrollably among animals but is quite nonepidemic in man.

The 1942 Report pointed out that major BW attacks on man would depend heavily on the use of agents capable of infecting through the air, by inhalation. If BW is to be directed as a "weapon of mass destruction" primarily against man, the dissemination of its agents through the air becomes one of its most important problems. This looks like the core of modern BW, the trick that will spell success or failure in its use as a major weapon. How could it be done? There is no published information bearing directly on this question. But there is some that bears on it indirectly, suggesting how it might be done—and, more significantly, showing that, on a small laboratory scale at all events, it can be done with conspicuous success.

General principles tell us that there must be more than one way of doing a job of this kind. The main problem is that of distributing a sufficiently high concentration of BW agent through a sufficient volume of air in such a form that it reaches its target while still active. The central difficulty is the instability of BW agents, their susceptibility to injury by drying, by exposure to the ultraviolet radiation of sunlight, and even by mechanical forces. Assuming that the agent could be stabilized sufficiently to keep it alive and active through the processes of production, packing, storage, and shipment, it becomes necessary to assemble it in a containing device which, at the elected time, will distribute it effectively and without excessive injury. It would probably not be enough just to drop it in a bottle or other simple container into a crowd of people, for the agent would not automatically be suspended in air as it might in water; most of it would be wasted, militarily speaking, in a heap or puddle on the ground. The agent would have to be dispersed without killing it directly into the air at the appointed spot. It would have to be spread at a suitable distance above ground, as evenly as possible and as widely as the amount of agent present warranted. This implies some kind of noninjurious propulsive force acting on a relatively small volume of agent so as to scatter it.

It would also be necessary for the original mass to be broken up during the scattering into particles small enough to do two things: to remain suspended in air and to be capable of penetrating the human nose. Large particles would either fall to the ground too quickly or would be stopped by the nasal barriers of hairs and narrow convoluted moist passages, so that they would not get down into the lungs. This question of the size of particles is of general interest to the subject of air-borne infection as a phase of public health, and it is known that the particle size required to do these two things is of the order of 10 microns or less.

Whether or not you can appreciate the intricacies of this undertaking—and there are some problems I forbear to mention to avoid overcomplicating it—I think you will agree that it does not sound easy. It might be possible to manage with the aid of explosives, using some of the more stable agents like anthrax spores. This would be tricky, to say the least, because of the high temperatures and great pressures generated by explosions, both of which would be likely to injure BW agents if not to kill them outright. Duffour, in an article on BW published in 1937, made the statement that the effective dissemination of bacterial spores by this means had been "proved"; but I have not seen any published information to substantiate his claim.

Another way of accomplishing this purpose might be by spraying or, to use a technically more precise term, "atomization." The difference is one of particle size. Atomizers, exemplified by the familiar little instruments used for perfume or for nasal antiseptics or mouth washes, produce a "fog," or "cloud," containing particles or droplets that range downward in size from about 60 or 70 microns; sprays start at this point and go up. Different kinds of atomizers vary in the characteristic size of the particles they put out. It is known that atomizers can easily be made that will put out a cloud of particles of the right size for offensive BW. It is also known that they can be used successfully with infective agents.

This information is contained in a lengthy and somewhat forbidding technical monograph entitled *Experimental Airborne Infection*, which sets forth in considerable detail the results of an investigation carried on at Camp Detrick during the war. The investigation dealt, among other things, with "the stability and infectivity for laboratory animals of airborne clouds" of a group of agents highly infective for man. To quote the blurb on the jacket: "Buildings and the selection of equipment are fully described, in addition to new techniques and data for use in the study of fundamental mechanisms involved in air-borne infections. This volume will be of interest to all students of respiratory infections and to those concerned with the field of experimental epidemiology." Since its origin at Camp Detrick is plainly indicated, the fact need surprise nobody that it will also be of interest to students of BW. And since I happen to have directed the investigation in question and to have written the monograph, I can speak of its contents with some authority, if without modesty.

The monograph deals, as I have suggested, with the production of "clouds" of highly infective agents, under conditions of safety to the operating personnel as well as to the neighbors; with all the equipment, tools, and gadgets needed to do this job, from the specially designed "cloud-chamber" building down to atomizers and cloud-sampling devices;

with methods of measurement applied to such clouds; with the problem of stabilizing agents and how it was met; and with the exposure of small laboratory animals to the clouds. It will be found duly recorded that every last one of the animals that were exposed to the clouds could be infected or killed with every infective agent tried, that this could be done repeatedly, and that the conditions under which it was done could be clearly defined and measured.

This was a small-scale investigation. The infective clouds were confined to "cloud chambers" with a capacity of about 100 gallons. The findings are not directly applicable to the field, still less to the much more complicated conditions of warfare. Nevertheless it is plain that within these limitations the job of disseminating highly infective agents successfully through the air can be done; and this suggests an opening through the neck of the BW bottle. No student of the technical problems of BW, here or abroad, will have needed me to tell him this, unless perhaps he has already found other and possibly better ways of doing the same thing.

The infective agents used in these studies were the bacilli of tularemia, of brucellosis of swine, of glanders, and of melioidosis, and several viruses of the so-called "psittacosis group"—psittacosis itself and some of its relatives. These germs may have constituted the hottest batch of bugs ever handled at one time by a single group of men; but they were handled safely.

Each kind of germ was investigated separately to learn how to stabilize it—to prevent the atomizer from killing it or from killing too much of it. For this purpose different substances were tried for their protective value to the atomized agent. With some of them, different methods of growing and preparing the agent were used to make it more stable. The glanders and melioidosis bacilli performed best when suspended for atomization in glycerin and broth, while the bacillus of brucellosis gave its best cloud yields in a mixture of dextrin and a commercial product of protein decomposition. The viruses did well enough in broth alone. The tularemia germ gave the most trouble. Dilute glycerin was the best of many substances tried for stabilizing it but was not very satisfactory. Yet so potent was this germ that, although an average of only 2 per cent of the bacilli survived the spraying process and reached their animal targets intact, it was a simple matter to have enough in excess present at the start so that every last exposed animal could be infected and killed by the cloud.

All the agents were injured to some extent during the process of preparing clouds of them but none so badly as the tularemia germ. The proportion of survivors ranged for the others from about 10 per cent for the glanders bacillus and one of the psittacosis-like viruses to 23 per cent for another virus and 26 per cent for *Brucella*. And, after most of this work was done, it was found by accident in studies with a harmless germ that by changing the way in which the atomizer was operated the "recovery" of the germ could be more than doubled. Time and the exigencies of war research permitted only one inconclusive attempt to apply this discovery to the infective agents. The results as a whole seemed satisfactory, but there is no reason to doubt that with further research they could be improved.

We need not entertain serious doubts, then, that the bottleneck problem of BW—the large-scale dissemination of airborne agents—is not beyond the ken of human genius. We may be sure that it can be solved, and if we are sure of it and proceed to mix that assurance in proper proportions with all the other things the published record tells us about BW, we need not doubt that BW is capable of taking its place beside the atomic bomb and other major weapons adaptable to mass destruction.

10. DEFENSE

THERE is so close a relationship between offense and defense in any kind of fighting that it is not easy to deal with either of them separately. The defender must know the weapon with which he is to be attacked, and the attacker must understand the defenses he expects to breach. If we are to defend ourselves against BW we must know all we can about the offensive side of it; and, conversely, the strategy and tactics of BW and the whole still-unanswered question of its ultimate effectiveness depend in part on questions of defense—on the kinds of things that can be done to ward it off and on how successful they are likely to be. But to the vast majority of us, perhaps to all except the military specialist whose job it is to wage war or to get ready to wage it, defense is the pulsating heart of the matter. We have no interest in making war, at least so long as we have a choice; but we have a deep and abiding interest in protecting ourselves against it. I hope this book will help to prevent outright the tragedy of another major war; but if it fails of this chief purpose, it should nevertheless have some use in helping us defend ourselves against BW. But let it be understood that defense will not be easy. I cannot promise to end this chapter on a hopeful note.

What we have called "bacteriology right side up" can help us here, although we must be careful in applying it. Like the sciences of medicine and public health and like the normal veterinary and agricultural sciences defensive BW is constructive in intent. It can make use of all that the peacetime sciences can teach it about the prevention, treatment, and control of infection, but that will be only the beginning. We may be sure in advance that the means available for dealing with natural phenomena will not suffice to deal with artificial ones.

The prevention, treatment, and control of natural infective diseases, particularly those of man, has by now reached a high state of development. Much that is known has been put into effective practice, at least in the more advanced countries. But even in such countries knowledge is far ahead of practice; applications lag everywhere, often disgracefully. In the United States we no longer have any cholera, and we have only rare isolated cases of plague. There are no more large outbreaks of typhoid fever, and yellow fever can be held to a minimum. But so far as know-how is concerned we could also wipe out syphilis and gonorrhea, which nevertheless remain scandalously prevalent; and we still have a lot of malaria which we cannot excuse on grounds of ignorance. Food-borne diseases, like dysentery and local outbreaks of typhoid fever, will continue to crop up as long as individuals suffer from them, excrete the germs, and remain careless about washing their hands. But the great water-borne epidemics and the great insect-borne diseases could both be cast out with the aid of available knowledge and skill from the two fields of biological science and engineering. To a large extent this has been done in countries like our own; but malaria control through the TVA hints at how much more might be done even here. The difficulties are not technical but political. And as for the major venereal diseases, the difficulties are again not technical. We know their causes: the gonococcus was one of the first of the disease-producing bacteria to be discovered, in 1879, and the spirochete of syphilis has been known since 1905. We know the manner of their spread. There are positive means for their prevention; we can detect them rapidly; and now, with the help of penicillin, we can cure them promptly. Yet they continue to be among the most prevalent and troublesome of all infections. The difficulties are not technical, but social, traditional, and probably in odd ways political.

This much needs to be said because it has a bearing on defense against BW. Our knowledge is great, but even in peace we apply it imperfectly. The impetus of war may prod us to do better, but we can hardly hope that any emergency will suddenly bring application abreast of knowledge.

And, even in peace, there is one large group of infections for which knowledge itself is deficient—the air-borne diseases: tuberculosis, influenza, the common cold; measles, mumps, and chicken pox; even meningitis, scarlet fever, and the pneumonias. There are moderately effective measures against some of these, like vaccines and other good methods for prevention and treatment of the individual person. But there is a common lack. We cannot control their transit through the air, as we can control typhoid by assuring a supply of clean drinking water or typhus by killing the body louse with DDT. It is not entirely a coincidence that the most important potential BW agents, as we have seen, are culled from this air-borne group.

So it is evident at the start that defensive BW is likely to be helped by the sciences of natural disease, but that the help, however great, will be limited. In its own field there are places where the path is clear and normal science walks upright with head high; but other places are full of boulders and underbrush, and here science limps painfully. Some of the most fertile areas of BW are contiguous with this rougher terrain. And beyond, BW has problems of its own.

The longer range problems of defensive BW are closely linked with the unsolved problems of public health. If anopheline mosquitoes with the plasmodia of malaria encysted in their little guts were to be planted in the Tennessee Valley, there is no reason to believe that they could take hold, that there would be any serious prevalence of malaria in man in the region. The waterways have deliberately been made inhospitable to the mosquito. Similarly it is very doubtful that cholera could be successfully implanted in any large American city, unless the city's highly developed water-purification system were first thoroughly disrupted.

But there are backward areas of our South that invite malaria or a spectacular increase of it; and in spite of DDT it must not be assumed that we are completely safe against other insect-borne diseases, like typhus or even bubonic plague. East of the Rocky Mountains plague is kept at bay almost entirely by a rigid ban on immigration of the plague bacillus, enforced by the unceasing vigilance of public-health officers in our ports. In war this barrier might well be overstepped. We have plenty of rats and fleas, again in spite of DDT and notwithstanding our wonderful new raticides. And in every city on our Eastern seaboard there are slums in which man and the flea-bitten rat compete for occupancy. Who is to say that plague could not take hold in such places if it were once introduced? And who can be certain that, if it once took hold, it would be content to prey on slum dwellers and not spread to the more refined side of the tracks? "It would seem foolhardy in the extreme," we said in the 1942 Report, "to suggest that the possible consequences of a bacterial attack in such areas of congestion can be dismissed lightly." The stresses and derangements of war might profoundly aggravate this problem of defense.

But frightening as these possibilities are, we are not defenseless against them. There are ways of dealing with water-borne and insect-borne diseases which make the prospect of disaster from them on the whole less formidable than that which might follow attacks with air-borne agents. It is with this group, against which our natural defenses are weak, that we have to reckon most seriously. And here it is not only the slum that invites contagion, although that invitation may be eloquent. It is the area of human congregation in general, clean as well as dirty, rich as well as poor, outdoors as well as indoors.

Contagion may strike from and through the air wherever crowds gather. In nature the great outdoors is salutary because the concentration of infective agent that comes from individual mouths and noses is never high and rarely very infective; the open sky is a beneficent diluter, and the sun's rays dry and sterilize quickly. But we have seen that in war BW agents deliberately discharged could be superlatively infective, highly concentrated, and protected against injury to themselves. By the air-borne route they would meet no effective man-made sanitary safeguards. The air is free in evil ways as well as in good ones.

Our long-range defenses are not strong. We could increase them by universal slum clearance, by unremitting war on rats and insect pests, by building TVA's wherever there is need for them, by air-conditioning schools, theaters, barracks, hospitals, office buildings, and by redesigning and rebuilding our housing units so as to disperse their huddled millions and give each of them plenty of clean air and sunlight. These measures could eliminate insect-borne disease, as measures that are now routine can eliminate large outbreaks of infection from contaminated drinking water. And if we could do all these things we would have very much less to fear from air-borne infection than we now have. They might, in fact, virtually eliminate such infections insofar as they arise from natural causes; but even such utopian operations could not be expected to eliminate the danger from airborne BW.

Our long-range defenses are not strong, and even utopian measures would leave them incomplete; but what of defense at shorter range? Our progress toward utopia will be painfully slow at best during the current period of crisis, and we shall have to muddle along as best we can, in war as in peace, with what we have. But if war were to bring BW tomorrow, what could we do to fend it off? This is the problem of defense as military men and other "realists" * see it, and we must try to look at it as they do.

Among these "realistic" defenses, some could be erected in advance, provided BW attacks were anticipated. Such preparatory defenses could be general—directed against BW as a whole or against large segments of it—or specific for individual agents, if anticipation could cover knowledge of the agent to be used by the enemy. But let us pass over this group of defenses temporarily in order to see what we would have to do if a BW attack came today.

The immediate problem would be to determine that the attack had taken place. The faster this could be done, the better our chances would be of mobilizing preventive and control measures. If we knew we had been attacked with a BW agent, we would also have to make all possible haste in identifying the agent. If we didn't find out what the agent was until symptoms of disease appeared, the attack would have been at least partly successful. But this double primary objective of BW defense—detection and identification—is likely to be formidable. BW agents as a class are imperceptible

---

* I have put the word "realists" in quotes because, beyond its formal definition in philosophy, I don't know exactly what it means. We are all realists, just as we are all liberals. Nobody admits to being a visionary or a reactionary; it is always the other fellow. Although I have myself branded some of my suggestions as "utopian" ("visionary" might have done as well), I am not persuaded that they are any less realistic than today's price of meat, which is fantastic.

to the senses. They cannot be seen in the environment or smelled or tasted or heard or felt. They do not respond to any established chemical or physical test.* At first detection might have to be sheer guesswork, based largely on negative considerations—an air attack, for example, that seemed to have no other recognizable purpose. Later, as experience with demonstrated BW attacks developed, their earmarks might come to be appreciated, and they might be spotted more easily. Yet the possibilities both of disguise and of variation—in agents, kinds of attack, and design of "munitions"—suggest that such experience would accumulate only very slowly, perhaps too slowly to be of much use. Here the insidious character and the great flexibility of BW would be conspicuous offensive advantages. The attacks might be masked as reconnaissance, as bombings with high explosive, or even as gas offensives. BW effects would become recognizable only after the incubation period of the agent had elapsed. Hence there would be manifest opportunities for confusion in defense, which the attacker would be likely to exploit fully.

Assuming, however, that we knew or thought a BW attack had occurred, we would have to make every effort to collect a sample of the agent to be used in identifying it. Either this would presuppose some knowledge of the character of the attack—whether via drinking water, infected vectors or animals, air, or otherwise—or else samples of many different

* The Merck Report states that "methods for the rapid and accurate detection of minute quantities of disease-producing agents" were developed in BW research during the war, but no details of such methods have been reported publicly. This official document also mentions "intensive investigations . . . on . . . physical and chemical protective measures" against BW, and makes the blanket statement that "adequate defenses against a potentially dangerous method of warfare were devised, [and] the possibility of surprise from this quarter was forestalled." Again no details have been released, and the reader will have to weigh these statements as best he can against the import of the present chapter, which, like the rest of this book, is of course based only on published information.

kinds would have to be collected for analysis. Air samples might give more trouble than others; to be useful they probably would have to be collected during the attack and not far from the center of it. While satisfactory equipment for this purpose is available, the chances would be against its being on hand and ready for use at the psychological moment. Once that moment had passed identification might have to wait until victims with symptoms of illness began to appear.

If a satisfactory sample could be obtained the procedure for identification of a BW agent in it would be straightforward, although far from simple. In only a few comparatively unimportant instances could the identification be made, even provisionally, within an hour or so after the sample reached a laboratory. This would be easiest if the sample consisted of infected insects or animals. But many provisional and most confirmatory identifying tests would require inoculation of experimental animals; and the time unavoidably consumed in waiting for the animals to get sick or to die would be likely to stretch beyond the incubation period for man. This would bring the result too late to be of any use in prevention.

During the early period of BW trials in war it seems most probable that both detection of the fact of an attack and identification of the offending agent would be made by hindsight—by established clinical and laboratory methods on sick people or on specimens of their tissues or fluids. If the process of defense were to begin at this point, it is obvious that the attack would have been successful; but the clinical diagnosis would have to be made in any event so that specific treatment might be prescribed if it were available and to permit the use of appropriate measures of public-health control. Here, however, another complication would enter.

Since a BW attack may be manifested only by the appearance of cases of illness under unusual circumstances, with no direct or clinching evidence of the actual attack—as in the alleged Japanese plague offensive in China in 1940—it is only too obvious that opportunities would arise for the wildest kind of rumor mongering. Naturally occurring outbreaks of disease might be attributed to BW, and actual attacks might pass unrecognized as such.

On October 12, 1947, the New York commentator and columnist Walter Winchell said over the air: "The Russians have developed germ warfare. The cholera plague in Egypt is suspected abroad of being a Soviet experiment. There are some very suspicious things about that plague in Egypt, although there's no positive evidence either way." There was indeed no positive evidence. I know nothing of Mr. Winchell's foreign sources, although they may possibly have come from Egypt itself, since that country, apparently BW-minded, has more recently leveled a formal accusation of the same sort but in another direction: this time it was Israel that was charged with waging BW, and the specific charge was the pollution of drinking water with typhoid and dysentery bacilli.*

Now it is true that the cholera epidemic in Egypt in the fall of 1947 was extremely serious. There were more than 20,000 cases and over 10,000 lives lost. It is also true that cholera had not been known in Egypt previously for forty-five years. The event thus had a superficial resemblance to the plague episodes in central China in 1940, although in Egypt, as far as I know, nobody reported seeing any Russian planes or saboteurs.† There are, however, certain additional and fundamental differences which to my mind completely discredit the

* The Egyptian statement (*PM*, May 28, 1948), read to the UN Security Council by Faris el Khouri of Syria, alleged a confession by two captured Zionists. The Israel representative at UN, Major Aubrey Eban, retorted that the charge was "the most depraved, medieval anti-Semitism."

† Certainly no such suggestion was made officially. In a World Health Organization report on the Egyptian epidemic, in fact, it is said that "firsthand observers think they can trace the origin of the infection to Egyptian laborers infected by aeroplanes coming from India." India is the principal world focus of cholera.

Egyptian rumor. The first is that serious experimenters with BW—and the Russians, if they have any interest in the subject, must be assumed to be serious about it—would be most unlikely to choose the germ of cholera as an agent. As I have pointed out elsewhere in this book, cholera is even less predictable than the bubonic form of plague, itself a poor BW choice. It is a fact that cholera suddenly appeared in serious form in Egypt, but all our knowledge of this disease supports the idea that it must have arisen by natural accident rather than by deliberate intent. Moreover, the Russians must be astute enough to realize that, if they were to launch an "experimental" BW attack for their own secret information, they could hardly have picked out a disease and a spot on the globe that would attract more immediate and more widespread attention throughout the world than cholera in Egypt. And if actual warfare were intended—as now seems highly unlikely—the Russians would hardly have been content with this isolated attack in what to them must have been a relatively unimportant quarter.

The point must be clear, nevertheless, that it may be hard to identify an outbreak of infective disease as a BW attack and that as a result an extremely fertile field is opened for the cultivation of rumors. This would certainly be true particularly during actual warfare and more particularly after there have been one or more events that look like BW or have been positively identified as such. The resulting aggravation of the difficulties of defense hardly needs further emphasis.

Let us assume, then, that a BW attack has in fact been made on a city and that the event has been sufficiently appreciated by the defenders to spur them to action. Whether the agent has yet been identified or not, and indeed, as soon as possible after the fact of the attack has been accepted, the machinery of defense must be put into motion. The problem is now one of epidemic or potentially epidemic disease in wartime, probably augmented by unfamiliarity with the malady if not by complete ignorance of its nature and accompanied by an electric awareness of the imminence of successive attacks, which may turn out to be similar or different.

If the target area can be delimited it may be placed under stringent quarantine in an effort to prevent infection from spreading beyond it. As casualties appear, the individuals will in all probability be isolated, so as to protect those in the attacked locality who may not have been exposed. Both of these measures—quarantine and isolation—will be more difficult to impose and more imperfect in their results in proportion to the severity of the attack, the amount of derangement of normal facilities caused by it, and the disorganization associated with other military activity or wartime conditions in the area. The quarantine is almost certain to be incomplete, for the target locality will hardly be entirely self-sufficient. Some intercourse with surrounding regions will be required, and leakage of the infection may be the consequence. If healthy carriers of the infection or persons during the incubation period are allowed to leave the area the disease may spread widely after they have entered unrestricted zones. Likewise isolation, although it must be tried, is likely to fail of its main purpose; for the infection will probably have been heavily seeded into the population, casualties will build up rapidly to a peak and then fall off as the limits of variation in incubation period are passed, but secondary cases may have been infected from the first batch before they had been recognized as casualties and isolated. Unless the attack is inherently weak or fails of itself, quarantine and isolation, especially if applied without full knowledge of the illness and its epidemic habits, are not likely to do much good.

But if the full machinery of defense were not already mobilized in anticipation of BW attacks, one successful attack would throw the switch and start all the wheels moving. At this point the veil of secrecy would have to be lifted sufficiently to allow civilian defense squads to be taught whatever might be known of means to detect a BW attack. They would need to know how they might recognize its munitions and be equipped with protective clothing so that they could approach them safely to sample their contents and if possible to put them out of action. Regional or mobile BW laboratories would be provided and equipped to carry samples through the process of identification. Special warning systems would be devised and protective shelters built; BW masks would be distributed. Sanitation teams would be organized for stepped-up inspection of water and food supplies and for routine and emergency sampling of water and air. Public-health and hospital facilities would be alerted and reconstituted and their stocks of diagnostic materials, vaccines, and remedies augmented. Private physicians and nurses would be mobilized; health officers, civilian or military, would be given increased power to order, control, or prevent mass evacuations or quarantines, to issue public directions or warnings, and to devise and issue propaganda to forestall disorder and demoralization.

Immediate defensive possibilities would now rest principally on four groups of means: on sanitation; on the use of masks and other physical barriers to infection; on vaccination and other biological protective measures; and on the treatment of casualties. How effective could we expect these means to be?

Sanitation is likely to be the most effective of the four. If its opportunity to function were not seriously interfered with by disruption of its facilities through bombing and if the people could be kept tractable and orderly, the machinery of sanitation should be able to prevent large-scale water-borne diseases and to make considerable headway against those spread by insects. Even if city water systems were partially disorganized, so long as drinking water could be made available it should not be too difficult to have it decontaminated by chlorination or boiling. These steps could be taken locally by groups ranging down to the individual family. Destruction of mosquitoes, lice, fleas, and ticks, and if necessary of rats and other rodents could be accelerated under emergency stress and made very successful—with slum areas perhaps excepted—given only public cooperation.

But, as I have suggested, sanitation of air is another matter. If the air were heavily polluted there would be no sure way of sterilizing it before it reached the lungs of those in the target zone. This would be particularly true of the open air and of private dwellings; so that protection of the great mass of the population, who would have to be in one or the other of these situations most of the time, would necessarily rely on a system of BW-raid warnings and on collective shelters. In public buildings of all kinds, wherever they might be feasible, steps toward air purification would be taken as far as the emergency might permit. Air conditioning is probably the best of these, using special germproof filter pads. But whether available facilities for this purpose could be materially increased under wartime conditions is doubtful. Ultraviolet lamps would be installed in public places to the limit of productive and distributive capacity; but their air-sterilizing value is usually incomplete and at best limited to rather small spaces. Their use also entails risks, especially of eye burns, which under wartime conditions might not be easily controlled. Installation of sprays and vaporizers for triethylene glycol and other air disinfectants would certainly also be expanded. These measures are useful in larger chambers than are ultraviolet lamps; they could even be used in a large theater that lacked air conditioning; but again they are likely to do an incomplete job of sterilizing the air, reducing the germ concentration but not eliminating it. The oiling of floors and other surfaces and the use of oiled vertical cloth barriers like curtains would be recommended and might have considerable, although certainly not unlimited, value in collecting and holding germ-laden dust. But all these measures put together could not be expected to have more than fractional usefulness in the sanitation of BW-polluted air.

We may take it for granted that reliable physical barriers to infection—germproof face masks, over-all protective clothing, and shelters provided with dependable filters—could be produced and made available. We may even assume that they would be available in sufficient quantity for the whole civilian population of large cities. Pictures of germproof coveralls developed for BW were released by the United States Navy early in 1946, and similar equipment has been described by Dr. James A. Reyniers, of Notre Dame University, in connection with his ingenious experiments on the rearing of germfree animals.* If every last man, woman, and child in an area attacked with an air-borne BW agent were at the proper time either wearing such a mask or safely installed behind filters in a shelter and if this state of affairs could remain undisturbed until decontamination squads in BW coveralls had cleaned up the mess and until the breeze had swept the air of the city clean—*if* all these things could be done without a break, the attack *might* be completely forestalled. Even so it might not be, for seepage of the virulent cloud through open windows and persistence of the agent beyond the supposedly dangerous interval might interfere.

* Germfree animals are obtained by taking them from the mother by aseptic surgery and rearing them with sterilized food in sterilized air. The tanks developed by Dr. Reyniers for this neat trick, equipped with sealed windows and gloves reaching inward, served as the "cloud chambers" in the Camp Detrick studies on air-borne infection. Dr. Reyniers's germfree animals do well enough inside their sterile tanks, but if taken outside, any passing germ, although ordinarily harmless, may kill them.

The main trouble here, however, would arise from the extreme improbability that *everyone* could be protected during the attack. It is hard to believe that so perfect a warning system could be devised and so rigid a discipline imposed that there would not be stragglers in large numbers. Face masks can't be worn all the time by anyone, still less by everyone. It is not even likely that every man, woman, and child would always have one ready at hand. Nor could everyone be expected to reach or to stay inside a collective protector until somebody in command decided to sound the all clear—itself a difficult decision. With a persistent agent or with stray contacts and a self-propagating agent, the attack might succeed in spite of the physical barriers applied after sufficient warning. The shelters would probably be fortified with ultraviolet lamps and other air-disinfecting equipment; but even so the late entrance of a few infected stragglers might play havoc with the crowd inside. We need not doubt that the attackers would appreciate all this and that it would be easier for offensive strategy to jump the barriers than for defense to erect them.

In addition, however, the population could be vaccinated; and if adequately vaccinated (you may say), it would have nothing to fear even though masks and shelters worked imperfectly and though sanitation broke down. If you think so and take comfort in the thought, I am sorry to have to disillusion you. Vaccination is a fence full of holes. There are good vaccines and fair ones and poor ones; and there are many infections against which we have no vaccines at all despite years of research directed toward making them. The diseases of man against which we have really good vaccines are so few that we can list them: smallpox, yellow fever, typhus fever, diphtheria, tetanus, and (probably) botulism. That is all. Useful, but at a lower level or more doubtful, are vaccines against rabies, influenza, some kinds of encephalitis,

Rocky Mountain spotted fever, typhoid and related fevers, whooping cough, and plague. Still more doubtful are those for cholera, the pneumococcal pneumonias, tuberculosis, and psittacosis. Others you may have heard of are either still experimental, highly controversial, or useless.

Only the vaccines in the first group can be thought of as strong enough to protect against the high dosages of infection likely to characterize BW attacks, and even with these there can be no guarantee that the dosages would not be high enough to overcome vaccine protection. There are only three putative BW agents in the group: yellow fever, typhus, and botulism.

In the second and third groups are vaccines that have great value in public-health protection, and some of them would doubtless be used for BW; but they would have little value as armor against germ bullets. The typhoid vaccines, for instance (like so-called TAB), have unquestioned protective value; but the protection they afford is only relative even in public-health practice. No health officer in his right mind would contemplate the relaxation of water sanitation merely because all his charges had been vaccinated; and no student of the history of typhoid fever doubts that sanitation deserves the major share of glory for the conquest of this disease in cities and among armies.

We have no satisfactory vaccines for human use against brucellosis, tularemia, glanders, melioidosis, anthrax—to name only a few. Some of these might be developed, and some existing vaccines—like that against plague—can probably be improved; but for the others nobody can promise that highly effective vaccines will ever be available. There may be limiting factors in the biological process of protection by vaccination that block this road toward the control of individual diseases.

And as BW extends beyond the uncharted frontiers of

public health it runs into another difficulty. To tell you about this I quote from the official report on BW issued to the United Nations by the United States State Department:

"It is quite probable that research directed toward enhancing the virulence of pathogenic microorganisms would result in the production of varieties much more virulent than those now known. The use of varieties of pathogenic microorganisms of such unusually high virulence might well overpower the means of protection now believed adequate. In addition, there is the probability that a variety of a known pathogenic agent, antigenically different from those varieties normally encountered, might be selected or developed. If this were done, the presently known immunizing agent would be ineffective against the newly selected or developed variety."

This means that a BW agent might be stepped up in potency so as to overcome methods of existing protection or altered so that the usual vaccine would not protect against it.

But if vaccination would give us less protection against BW than some of us may have thought, what of the new wonder drugs that have changed the face of medical practice in recent years? Could not the sulfa drugs, penicillin, streptomycin, and the others be given out *before* a BW attack so as to safeguard us? They could, and no doubt they would. Within limits they most certainly would be very useful. But they have their limits.

Thus far the range of known drugs falls considerably short of the range of infections; many of the virus diseases, in particular, are not covered. But let us not labor the point. Current indications are very hopeful. This is a very fertile and highly lucrative field, and it is now being tilled with extraordinary enthusiasm. Let us shelve our doubts and assume that by the time BW comes we shall have good drugs for every infection. And let us not quibble but assume further that there would never be any shortage of needed drugs. How would they be likely to work out in practice, and how much benefit could we expect from them?

The problem here is much like that of masks and other physical barriers. It is a question of having our guard up when the punch comes and of keeping it up long enough. It is not possible that all of us could be kept continuously hopped up with sulfa drugs, penicillin, streptomycin, and a few or many other drugs. If we knew for sure that on Friday the thirteenth at 1300 hours there would be an attack over Area A of City B with Agent X, the whole population of the area might be given a whopping dose of Drug Y at 1200 hours and the attack might be circumvented. But if the enemy switched to Agent Z or attacked at 1100 or at 1800, the population might be out of luck. The effect of these drugs usually lasts only a few hours, seldom more than one day. After that the dosage must be repeated, again and again. Some people are sensitive to one or more of the drugs and can't take them at all. The more widely and the more often the drugs were used, the more people would become sensitive to them. And some germs are, become, or can be made "fast" to a drug so that it does not hurt them. As BW agents might be stepped up in virulence or altered to make them proof against vaccines, they might also be manipulated so that the wonder drugs would act on them like so much sugar candy.

The problems of treatment, once casualties had developed, would be much the same. Be it noted that the appearance of BW casualties would mark the success of the attack; the major defenses would already have been overcome. Here again we may assume a drug for every disease and enough of it. And we need not doubt that modern treatment has it in its power greatly to mitigate the consequences of BW. Because of it cases would be milder, and deaths would be fewer. But too much optimism over effective treatment is hardly warranted. Good treatment is an unmixed blessing to the sick and undoubtedly generates more gratitude toward doctors than all the means of prevention and public-health control put together. But treatment can rarely solve a public-health problem, and it cannot solve the problem of defense against BW. Once the sick appear the attack will have achieved its purpose; and, indeed, if by living on and recovering unscathed the casualties help to tie up hospital facilities and personnel and in other ways, directly or indirectly, interfere with or cripple the normal activity of the community, the enemy may like it better than if they had been killed outright.

This is the picture, as I see it, of defense against BW agents that cause disease in man. What of animals and plants? For the most part the problems here are even more difficult. Animals and plants cannot cooperate in anticipating BW attacks; they cannot easily wear masks or be moved to shelters. For neither group can there be any sanitation worth speaking of. Plants cannot be vaccinated. Animals can be, and vaccines might be somewhat more effective for animals than for men because more vaccines could be used, including certain ones, like the Pasteur vaccine for anthrax, whose use may entail some risk of injury or death. Other preventive measures and methods of treatment would have distinctly less value. It is usually economically more practicable to destroy sick animals or plants intended for human use than to attempt any large-scale treatment of them. The defenses here are pitiably weak.

But then, I think you must agree, defense against BW as a whole is pitiably weak, so weak that none of us, civilian or military, can find much comfort in its prospect. To the military, for BW as for all other modern weapons, defense must be pushed for all it is worth, but it isn't worth much. For BW as for the others, from the military viewpoint, the best defense will be offense—retaliation in kind, if possible doubled and redoubled. I hope you can find some comfort in this thought; it leaves me very cold.

11. INTERNATIONAL CONTROL

A FEW short years after the end of the greatest war in history we face again the threat of a still greater war. In that war, if it comes, BW is likely to be used along with all other "major weapons adaptable to mass destruction." That BW is such a major weapon seems clear. It is flexible: diverse in its means of destruction, varied in its range of strategic and tactical uses. Its agents are surpassingly powerful; yet they are universally available, cheap, and easy to make, so that no nation can hope to have a monopoly of them. Its practicability is not proved and cannot be proved unless BW is used in war; but there is little doubt that it would be effective. The consequences of its widespread use are incalculable and might be irremediable. There seem to be no adequate defenses against it.

Even as I write, the clouds of war hang ominously over Berlin, and it seems only too sure that there or elsewhere they will not soon be dissipated. The outlines of BW are visible to me in those clouds, and it is urgent that something be done about them. But what can we do about clouds? It is unheard of, you may say, to think of dissipating them. Yet in the life of a scientist, every day brings news that was unheard of yesterday, and the march of the years and centuries has all but cast the word "impossible" out of our vocabulary. As God helps those who help themselves, we—you and I—

must search for a way to avert this storm—or risk being destroyed by it.

What kind of way can we look for? I can think of two, a specific one, which would be the better if it could be opened and traversed, and a more general one that we may hold in reserve. The road to peace is forked. One branch, which looks like the easier, leads through the international control of mass weapons. It has been explored for the atomic bomb, but the explorers have come to an impasse. We must retrace their steps and try to find out why they failed to get through and whether it is possible to do so with BW. If not, we shall have to come back and try the other branch, even though it looks forbidding. We have nothing to lose by trying, and a world at peace to gain.

We must digress, then, and talk for a while about atomic bombs.

On August 6, 1945, President Truman announced to the world that an American airplane had dropped a bomb on Hiroshima, a bomb that "had more power than 20,000 tons of TNT. It had more than 2,000 times the blast power of the British 'Grand Slam,' which is the largest bomb ever yet used in the history of warfare." He went on to say that "it is not intended to divulge the technical processes of production or all military applications" of this atomic bomb "pending further examination of possible methods of protecting us and the rest of the world from the danger of sudden destruction" and that "I shall give further consideration and make further recommendations to the Congress as to how atomic power can become a powerful and forceful influence toward the maintenance of world peace." Thus the Atomic Age began officially, and thus was introduced the most awesome question the peoples of the world have had to answer in their long history: now that we can compete with the sun in releasing energy, how are we going to keep from getting burned?

The decision to use the bomb was a closely reasoned one, as Henry L. Stimson, who as Secretary of War carried a major responsibility for making it, has ably pointed out. By hindsight it appears to have been inevitable. At all events a decision to withhold the bomb once it was available would have shattered all military precedents. Yet in June of 1945, before the first bomb was exploded at Alamogordo, a group of atomic scientists in Chicago, knowing of the bomb and cognizant of its potentialities, pleaded with Washington to withhold it or to explode it publicly and with due warning in an uninhabited spot. Albert Einstein, whose equation for the conversion of mass into energy was the primary basis of the bomb and who had been largely instrumental in having work on it started, said in London in August of 1946 that "he was sure that President Roosevelt would have forbidden the atomic bombing of Hiroshima had he been alive and that it was probably carried out to end the Pacific war before Russia could participate." * The decision to use the bomb had been made tentatively before Alamogordo; and one of the reasons Mr. Stimson has given for deciding to use it without warning on an inhabited target in Japan was the fear that the bomb might be a dud.

Hiroshima was blasted, and then Nagasaki. One bomb could be a fluke, but two would convince all doubters. Japan surrendered, and the United States became the greatest military power of all time or, by the same token, the most fearful of potential aggressors. The world stood aghast, awed, filled with a new and profound respect for a great country and its powerful science. The scientists, prepared as they had tried

* The British physicist, P. M. S. Blackett, in his *Military and Political Consequences of Atomic Energy* (Turnstile Press, London, 1948), which appeared while the present work was in press, devotes a chapter to an analysis of this question and concludes "that the dropping of the atomic bombs was not so much the last military act of the second world war, as the first act of the cold diplomatic war with Russia now in progress."

to be for the dramatic consequences of their work, were shocked out of their traditional detachment. But the Russians, perhaps both stunned and piqued after their own prodigious war effort, spoiled the show with their petulance, to our utter exasperation. The opening of the Atomic Age was magnificent, but there is no doubt that something went wrong in the first act.

That our leaders had qualms is not to be doubted. Any lesser new weapon would hardly have been handled like this one. President Truman announced its nature immediately, while en route home from Potsdam; and Secretary Stimson, on the same day, issued a more detailed statement on the background of the bomb, concluding with the promise that "every effort is being bent toward assuring that this new weapon and the new field of science that stands behind it will be employed wisely in the interests of the security of peace-loving nations and the well-being of the world." The amazingly detailed Smyth Report, prepared in advance, was released almost at once. Later both General Groves, who wrote the foreword to the report, and Mr. Lilienthal, after he had replaced the general, considered its publication to have been a mistake. On October 27 President Truman spoke of the bomb as our "sacred trust." On November 6 Mr. Molotov scoffed at "the secret," hinted darkly of anti-Soviet blocs forming in Western nations, and reassured the Russians that "we will have atomic energy and other things, too."

It was in this atmosphere that the UN Atomic Energy Commission was born. First concretely proposed at Washington in the Truman-Attlee-King Declaration of November 15, 1945, it was conceived a month later at the Three-Power Conference in Moscow and delivered January 24, 1946, in a resolution passed by the UN General Assembly without a dissenting vote. The wording of the terms of reference of the Commission (UNAEC) was given in the American-British-Canadian statement of November and continued through the others. The UNAEC was "to make specific proposals:

"*a.* For extending between all nations the exchange of basic scientific information for peaceful ends;

"*b.* For control of atomic energy to the extent necessary to insure its use only for peaceful purposes;

"*c.* For the elimination from national armaments of atomic weapons and of all other major weapons adaptable to mass destruction;

"*d.* For effective safeguards by way of inspection and other means to protect complying States against the hazards of violations and evasions."

Early in January Secretary of State Byrnes had appointed a committee to study means for the international control of atomic energy, and on March 16, 1946, the Acheson-Lilienthal Report gave the world its detailed plan toward this end. As the letter of transmittal by the Acheson Committee to Mr. Byrnes quoted with approval the words of the Lilienthal Board's Report, it was submitted "not as a final plan, but as a place to begin, a foundation on which to build." But when Mr. Baruch presented the official U.S. proposals at the first meeting of the UNAEC on June 14, 1946, the plan was recognizably the same except for the added demand that the "veto" —the unanimity rule among the Great Powers—be abolished as far as atomic energy was concerned. And during two years of wrangling in the UNAEC, the U.S. plan was altered in no essential point; the "place to begin" became the place to end; the "foundation" solidified into the final structure, with no house on it. While stubbornness battered in frustration against obstinacy, the cherished crystal of peace sank into a deliquescence of mutual recrimination. The body of the UNAEC was pronounced dead on May 17, 1948, with a confession of failure and a vote to suspend. It was buried on June 22 in the Security Council, when Mr. Gromyko cast his twenty-sixth veto to kill the majority plan for international control. A ghost of the Commission waits upon the General Assembly.*

Who killed the UNAEC? Not I, said Mr. Baruch, Mr. Austin, and Mr. Osborn, it was those obstinate Russians. Not I, said Mr. Gromyko, Mr. Molotov, and Mr. Vishinsky, it was those greedy Americans. It may have been a little of both; but it doesn't matter very much *who* did. What matters is *how* it died and *why*. It seems to me that the baby was ill conceived, sickly from birth, and foredoomed to an early death. It hadn't a chance.

It hadn't a chance for two reasons. One is that the attempt to approach the great problem of peace through the control of one weapon—even though it be far and away the most potent of all weapons—could not have succeeded while other mass weapons, remaining uncontrolled, left the prospect of a devastating war essentially unmitigated. Although the UNAEC was directed to make proposals on "all other weapons adaptable to mass destruction," it never considered anything but atomic energy. Mr. Baruch, it is true, said that "before a country is ready to relinquish any winning weapons . . . it must have a guarantee of safety, not only against the offenders in the atomic area, but against the illegal users of other weapons—bacteriological, biological, gas—perhaps —why not?—against war itself. . . . If we succeed in finding a suitable way to control atomic weapons, it is reasonable to hope that we may also preclude the use of other weapons

---

* The ghost rattled its dry bones at Paris in October, 1948, in the Political Committee of the UN Assembly, where Mr. Austin and Mr. Vishinsky held forth much as usual. On November 4 the whole Assembly, by a vote of 40 to 6 (with India, South Africa, Afghanistan, and Venezuela abstaining), approved the Commission's majority plan for control, expressed official concern at the impasse between Russia and the West, asked the Big Five plus Canada to seek a basis of agreement, and told the UNAEC to keep working. All this happened after the present book had gone to press and hardly warrants any change in its text. According to the Assembly, the UNAEC is still alive, but even doctors have been known to disagree.

adaptable to mass destruction. When a man learns to say 'A' he can, if he chooses, learn the rest of the alphabet, too."

The laudable piety of this suggestion, however, never came out of Sunday school into cold daylight; and even though our official 195-page statement of scientific information to the UNAEC contains 7 pages on BW, nothing ever came of it. The Polish-commission delegate, Zlotowski, did indeed propose to raise the BW question before the UNAEC in October, 1947; but if it was raised no action was taken on it. If a discussion of BW control was aborted because it looked even more difficult than atomic energy—we shall examine this matter of difficulty more closely later—my point that this road to peace was closed would be all the more gloomily confirmed.

The other reason why the UNAEC could not but fail was the atmosphere of mistrust and suspicion in which it had to work. The American proposals were doomed politically because, doubtless for good and sufficient reasons, they were expressive of fear and an excess of caution; and the Russian counterproposals, no doubt for equally compelling reasons, were evasive, nebulous, and implausible. Or, to put the matter differently, neither of the two principal negotiators nor any of the lesser participants who gave us our consistent but dubious majority could act entirely in good faith for the simple reason that there was no faith. The dubious majority continually escaped from reality into technology, and the Russians, possibly more realistic than the rest but no less frustrated, continually abstained or vetoed. Neither side ever met the other halfway. But we had the bombs, the know-how, and the consistent majority; and the Russians were utterly exasperating.

Someday I hope the full story will be written, objectively as it needs to be and fully documented. It might be written today by Trygvie Lie or a man from Mars but by nobody else that I know of. My own view, which is certainly not unbiased, has been formed during a day-to-day study of the whole play as it unfolded via at least the major speeches and documents. I have been sustained in it by a search for parallels between atomic warfare and biological warfare, as well as by the hope which the world must have shared that somehow this desperate experiment might not fail. It is not possible in a book like this to document my opinion fully, but let's look at a few exhibits.

I have said that the American plan was expressive of fear and an excess of caution. Consider this passage from the Acheson-Lilienthal Report:

"The scheduling will determine the rapidity with which a condition of international balance will replace the present position. Once the plan is fully in operation it will afford a great measure of security against surprise attack; it will provide clear danger signals and give us time, if we take over the available facilities, to prepare for atomic warfare. The significant fact is that at all times during the transition period at least such facilities will continue to be located within the United States. Thus should there be a breakdown in the plan at any time during the transition, we shall be in a favorable position with regard to atomic weapons."

Picture Mr. Molotov, reading.

And the U.S. proposals airily assumed that the whole world would accept the rectitude of "the American way." From the same source:

"The problem of power-producing piles should be somewhat less difficult in the case of nondangerous piles. In these, fissionable materials will be denatured. The charter should be able to provide for their allocation of this type of plant in accordance with more conventional economic standards. It might be possible to provide that they should be located on the basis of competitive bids among interested nations."

The Baruch proposals retained both these thoughts in different words. They provided that the U.S. would discontinue the manufacture of atomic bombs only "when an adequate system for control of atomic energy, including the renunciation of the bomb as a weapon [by everybody else?] had been agreed upon and put into effective operation and condign punishments set up for violations of the rules of control which are to be stigmatized as international crimes. . . ."

They also provided that "the Authority should exercise complete managerial control," that it should "operate all plants producing fissionable materials in dangerous quantities" and "own and control the products of these plants." And, after such control had been provided for, "there should be as little interference as may be with the economic plans and the present private, corporate, and state relationships in the several countries involved."

On June 19 Mr. Gromyko tried, I do not know how hard, to find words to express the Russian distaste. He came up with these among others:

"One of the fundamental elements of the existing situation is characterized by the absence of any kind of limit to the production and application of atomic weapons. These elements are important considerations and only strengthen the suspicion existing between countries and worsen relations between them, calling forth political instability. It is clear that a continuation of this situation is likely to bring only negative results for the peace of the world."

There is surely something more here than the defects of translation from the Russian.

A year later Mr. Gromyko continued to dance lightly around his objections instead of stating them flatly:

"The Soviet Union cannot agree that its national economy be made dependent on the will even of a majority in the control organ, being aware that such majority may take one-sided decisions. The Soviet Union cannot subject the fate of its national economy to dependence on the will of the majority in such an international organ, because it realizes that there may be decisions dictated not only by interests of justice."

It is said twice, but it is still not said.

In October, 1946, Mr. Molotov had spoken more bluntly:

"The American plan, the so-called 'Baruch plan' . . . is based on the desire to secure for the United States the monopolistic possession of the atomic bomb. At the same time, it calls for the earliest possible establishment of control over the production of atomic energy in all countries, giving to this control an appearance of international character but, in fact, attempting to protect in a veiled form the monopolistic position of the United States in this field. It is obvious that projects of this kind are unacceptable. . . ."

And Mr. Molotov, further along in the same speech, did a little veil dance of his own:

". . . it should not be forgotten that atomic bombs used by one side may be opposed by atomic bombs and something else from the other side. . . ."

These few excerpts from official statements of the two principal camps will have to serve. Hundreds of thousands of additional words have been spoken and written on the subject, but for me at least they have added no further clarity to it. They have, indeed, tended to befog it in clouds of diplomatic verbiage and to mire it ever more deeply in the marsh of technological irrelevance. The American plan possessed technical ingenuity of a very high order. In a political vacuum it would have commanded the unreserved admiration that one accords to genius operating strictly within its own sphere. But this is a political and economic problem, not purely a scientific one. Science might have helped it but could not dominate it or solve it out of its larger context. The basic disagreement was a conflict of national philosophies and its resulting mutual distrust and suspicion. In this atmosphere no agreement on essentials was possible, and agreement on technical matters alone would have been meaningless.

Among the many autopsy reports on the UNAEC that have appeared and doubtless will continue to appear I choose two examples for brief comment.

The first report, in the sober and authoritative *Bulletin of the Atomic Scientists*, is by Edward A. Shils, associate professor in the Committee on Social Thought at the University of Chicago and Reader in Sociology at the London School of Economics, who lays chief blame for failure at the door of the Soviet Union, although not without qualification. He charges the Russians with having failed *(a)* to prepare themselves adequately on the technical side of the problem; *(b)* to appreciate the great significance of the atomic bomb; and *(c)* to understand what they call the "bourgeois world" and therefore *(d)* to credit the basic generosity of the majority proposals. All these ideas and the manner in which they are developed read to me like dream stuff, in which shreds of reality are so entangled with long strands of fancy and possibly of wish fulfillment that it would take a skillful Freudian to unravel them. This paper could not be more replete with self-righteous premises, offered with neither substantiation nor apology—the "everybody knows" sort of thing—if it had been written by an average Congressman. Nevertheless Mr. Shils admits, although without great emphasis, that the majority failed to make all reasonable concessions—on the timing of "stages" in the evolution of the control scheme, on the veto, and on the prohibitory convention which the Russians demanded as a basis for negotiation. And, despite his staunch and wholehearted support of the American position, Mr. Shils includes one remarkably divergent paragraph which I quote in full:

"As the expectation of agreement declined almost to nothingness and as irritation with the Soviet delegates grew within the Commission, the American zeal to have the majority control scheme realized also seemed to decline, being replaced by the desire to utilize the morally advantageous position for propaganda purposes. It is not meant here that an agreement on control along the proposed lines had become undesirable to the Americans—although it might have become that had the Soviet Union during the last months of the Commission's life suddenly come out in favor of the majority scheme! It is rather meant that as time went on, the immediate objective seemed to be to prevent the Soviet Union from 'getting away with anything.'"

The second autopsy report, the United States State Department's "informal summary" of the life and death of the UNAEC, blames the Russians with no qualifications whatsoever. Perhaps it is unavoidable that our government take the position that its behavior is immaculate. To a scientist, indeed, the apparently insuperable obstacle that prevents governments from admitting error, except that made by other governments, measures the yawning gulf between science and public affairs. A scientist knows that only pure mathematics can be without error. There is error in filling a test tube, in reading a meter, in using words to express thought, and in thought itself. Error must be recognized and wherever possible measured; for science to deny its existence would be fatal. And in the end it may prove equally fatal for governments to do so. To err is human, we say; yet we alone among peoples do not err. It is quite unimaginable to me that our State Department could hope not to defeat its own ends when, in a section labeled "Semantics and Propaganda," it attributes misunderstanding, confusion, and doubtful motives to the Russian side alone. On the other hand it seems to me unnecessary to look further for the roots of failure in the UNAEC. Negotiation implies compromise, and compromise is give-and-take. We and our dubious majority seem to have demanded of the Russians something dangerously close to unconditional surrender. But they appear to be a proud people like ourselves.

The UNAEC failed, but in so doing it left unanswered two questions to which we must now return. The first of these may be phrased thus: If it had been possible to secure international agreement at the political level, would the American plan for the technological control of atomic energy have been practicable? And, secondly: Could any comparable scheme be expected to work for the international control of BW?

I have already offered the opinion, which I share with most others, that the U.S. plan for international control was a work of technical genius. As this plan was formulated in the Acheson-Lilienthal Report, transmitted in the Baruch proposals, and elaborated in Part II of the Second Report of the UNAEC and the Annex to its Third Report, it is a thing of beauty, albeit not fully in accord with modern principles of functionalism in design. It is like a full-scale sailing vessel built in the sub-basement of a skyscraper in an inland city. There would seem to be little doubt that it would float and sail, if only it could be brought to navigable water and launched.

The practicability of the plan hinges on the unique characteristics of large-scale atomic-energy development: on the use of uranium and thorium ores as sole raw materials and on the close parallelism, up to an advanced state of manufacture, of destructive and peaceful developments. It takes advantage of the opportunities for effective inspection which inhere in the need of such developments for massive installations, highly developed industrial capacity, and large accumulations of skilled personnel. It therefore provides for an international agency that would maintain effective ownership and control of the raw materials and their products from mining through the stages of their manufacture, and including arrangements with individual nations to oversee the discovery of new deposits. And it spells out in detail the steps and provisions necessary for the maintenance and exercise of such control by the agency, including "unimpeded right of ingress, egress, and access to the extent necessary to carry out the powers and duties of the agency." It is a bold and challenging plan; and if only the world were ready for it I have no doubt that it could be made to work.

The world is obviously not ready for it, and therefore it may be slightly academic to inquire whether any comparable plan could be devised for BW. But we must make the inquiry nevertheless.

From the characteristics of BW as they have been detailed in preceding chapters it appears that useful parallels between germs and atomic nuclei as weapons are few indeed. Whereas the military development of nuclear energy depends upon two raw materials that are comparatively scarce, restricted in their occurrence, and very expensive, the raw materials of BW are manifold, ubiquitous, and virtually without cost. If atomic bombs are to be made by individual nations they demand a wealthy country, industrially highly developed, with abundant power supplies and a plenitude of highly skilled personnel. But the nature of BW indicates that it could be developed by small poor countries as well as large rich ones, that its cost would be low, its material requirements few, and its demands for personnel only such as could be met wherever there are modern engineering, medical, veterinary, and agricultural-science facilities. In 1946 it seemed safe to assume that the United States had a monopoly on the means and know-how for atomic-bomb production. While this assumption becomes increasingly less tenable as time goes on, a parallel assumption for BW has never been tenable. It may be that other countries are more advanced than we in BW development.

There is no good reason to believe that we have a monopoly of biological weapons. As to whether the Russians have BW, there have been no well-authenticated reports but several hints and rumors, some of which leave little doubt that they have been interested in it for a long time. LeRenard has alleged that after the disclosures regarding German BW at the end of World War I, "the U.S.S.R. installed on the shores of the Caspian Sea a military bacterial station for experimentation." Joseph E. Davies, in *Mission to Moscow*, states that some of the minor defendants in the "treason trials" of 1937–1938 were shown to have planned BW sabotage under German and Japanese direction. Maurice Hindus, the writer and lecturer, is quoted as having said in Montreal in January, 1948, without supporting detail, that "it was an ascertained fact that Russia was employing German scientists in bacteriological-warfare research. . . ." In March, 1948, an AP dispatch quoted Senator Edwin C. Johnson of Colorado as having asserted that the Russians have perfected a new weapon "far more effective than the atomic bomb—bacteriological warfare. Authorities I regard as reliable tell me the Russians have perfected this terrible warfare weapon of spreading plagues and germs. It will be far easier to use than the atomic bomb."

Russian official spokesmen, notably Mr. Gromyko, have mentioned BW on several occasions (for instance, on February 14, 1947, before the UN Security Council). It is expressive of Russian interest in the subject that on July 28, 1948, the Soviet Army newspaper, *Red Star*, described a Japanese BW station in World War II near Harbin, Manchuria, whose "capacity was nearly a ton of bubonic-plague bacteria a month" and which "used prisoners for tests, usually killing them in the process." In view of the known Russian activity in the development of other new weapons we had better assume that they are actively interested in BW.

There are additional points of contrast between BW and atomic energy. The production of atomic bombs might be controlled through international inspection and policing because large-scale development of fissionable products requires installations of a unique sort which offer only limited opportunities for disguise. But the facilities required for BW differ hardly at all from those used all over the world in peacetime research and industry; the possibilities for disguise and subterfuge, for hiding military activity under a cloak of normal science and production, are legion. For a system of inspection and policing to be effective in controlling BW it would seem unavoidable that it enter intimately into the medical, public-health, industrial, and related activities upon which the daily life and welfare of nations depend. Such control, it seems to me, would have to reach down so deeply into the personal lives of individuals throughout the world as to be possible only with the most highly centralized kind of world state—far more tightly organized, to be sure, than any world government suggested by present-day theorists. Quite aside from the practicability or impracticability of achieving such a state, it appears plain that it would be undesirable because the resulting security would not be worth its cost in sacrifice of personal freedom, however this moot word may be defined. But let's not anticipate the substance of the next chapter.

Historically the attempts up to now toward international control of mass weapons may be called, as Mr. Hoover said of prohibition, an "experiment noble in purpose." Doubtless they are worth further examination, for if an opening could be found through what looks like the blind end of this road into the sunlit field of peace it would be well worth the time and effort expended. Yet even if such an opening could be found for atomic energy, the indications are that it would lead only into a second and more impenetrable cul-de-sac for BW. From where I stand it seems best now that we return and try the other fork in the road.

12. THE LARGER PROBLEM

ON the third anniversary of Hiroshima the world slumped in moral depression and vented its half-hidden fears and feelings of guilt in international grouchiness. In the United Nations all efforts to approach peace through disarmament had bogged down. The Commission set up in a more hopeful time to give us international control of atomic bombs and other mass weapons had confessed failure, and progress toward the control of "conventional armaments" and an international security force had come to a standstill. World War II had submerged all but two contenders for global hegemony; and these two, in militarily muscle-bound pugnacity, were proceeding to divide the earth into two training camps for the greatest championship finish fight of all time. The smaller countries, finding the prospect of getting out of the way uncomfortably gloomy in the newly contracted spherical geography, hastened to pledge loyalty to one camp or the other. And the little people, caught up in their own daily problems of short housing and high prices, turned from the remote frustrations of international strife, in America to the sport pages and the comic strips, and abroad to whatever the national equivalents of these diversions may have been.

Breakdown in the UN Atomic Energy Commission was not the cause of failure elsewhere but the symbol. The Commission could not have succeeded because of fear; and even if by a miracle it had achieved its objective of sequestering all atomic bombs in some United Nations back yard it could not have accomplished its larger purpose of preventing war so long as fear had other weapons to play with. We were afraid to stop making the bombs until the world both agreed not to start making them and proved to our satisfaction that it was not doing so. The Russians were afraid to trust our generosity, even though nearly all the neighbors assured them of our good intentions. But the American control scheme, which everyone but the Soviets agreed was a work of technical genius, was tailored to fit the unique contours of atomic energy alone. Neither this nor any other known or imagined protective cloak could be expected to fit the other giants of mass destruction—like biological warfare—which lurked menacingly in the shadows of military secrecy.

The international control of atomic energy is not synonymous with peace. The world needs such control in order to encourage the peaceful development of atomic power, to make sure that its magnificent promise is fulfilled. But control will have to be a product of peace rather than a basis for it. Nor can we hope for peace through the control of other weapons, mass or minuscule. The Lilienthal-Baruch plans for atomic energy grew out of fear, were scaled to fear's dimensions, and were defeated by fear. The other weapons, BW in particular, do not lend themselves to any such control scheme; and even if a scheme could be devised for them it would be even more certain to fail while fear dominates the conference tables.

The road to peace is forked. One branch leads through the international control of weapons but is blocked by fear. Someday we shall have to lift the blockade and follow that branch home; but the barrier will have to be breached from behind, and to get to it we shall have to explore the other branch. From here this other branch looks rugged and formidable; but it seems to be the only path to peace.

As a specialist in a small field of science I might hesitate to offer my services as a guide but for one thing. A scientist is no better than other men and usually no worse. His opinions on matters within his own sphere merit the respect of those who have fewer facts than he; but in all other areas they are like the opinions of other men. A scientist may nevertheless have one kind of skill that need not be limited to his own specialty. He may know how to frame a problem and thus to take the first purposeful step toward solving it. His method of dealing with problems is the essence of science. It lends validity to the generic word "science," where otherwise there would be only dissimilar fragments like "mathematics," "physics," and "biology." It makes it possible to call a man a "scientist" even though he is not yet dead and implies no broader connotation and no deeper obeisance than we convey with the words "musician," "draftsman," or "administrator." Each, if he is worthy of the name, has a special skill that is broader than the field in which he elects to practice it.

The late war taught certain men to call themselves "scientists" where previously they had been shy. Necessity lifted them out of their own familiar laboratories and transplanted them into quite unfamiliar soil, where they learned, maybe with some surprise, that the method they had used to deal with familiar problems at home was equally effective in dealing with quite unfamiliar problems far afield. Thus a crystallographer could plan and carry out the evacuation of cities, and a geneticist could derive a formula for estimating the number of casualties to be expected from a bombing. Some of the world's most abstruse thinkers made an atomic bomb, and a group of gentle healers turned germs into weapons.

Problems are problems. Some are small and easy, others large and difficult; but all problems have a common quality.

If they can be visualized, they can be formulated; and if they can be formulated, there is at least a chance that they can be solved. This idea is basic to the philosophy of science and the first principle of its method. A scientist is one who understands this principle and knows how to apply it. It matters little in what field of human competence the problem lies, provided only that the scientist can come to understand the data in that field and to appreciate any special attributes or techniques it may require.

The scientist, moving from one field to another, does not usually invade an established field of science that is foreign to him—not that he might not do so but that the new field is already well occupied. The greatest scientists break new ground and open new fields to scientific inquiry, as did Newton, Darwin, Pasteur, and Einstein. Lesser ones may enter a field previously known but not well tenanted with scientists. Politics is such a field. Like medicine it has both its scientists and its practitioners; but, unlike medicine, politics is fairly obviously not being dealt with very well; whence the sad state of the world.

A scientist from another field, moreover, may enter politics in either of two ways, but not in both. If in so doing he abandons the methods of science and adopts the traditional methods of politics he must not be surprised to find himself being received like any other politician. There need be no harm in this—it is surely the scientist's privilege as a citizen and a human being to adopt such an approach if he wishes—and only the individual scientist can decide whether it can be justified by its possible rewards. On the other hand the scientist may attempt to apply the method of science to visualize and formulate the problems of politics as a means toward their solution. That is what I propose to attempt with the greatest problem of them all—the problem of peace.

It must be clear, then, that the next few pages do not contain The Answer, all in a little package neatly wrapped and tied. They contain rather a scientist's view of the contours and limits of the problem, of its area and topography. I have chosen to frame it with the aid of certain questions arranged with a view to helping you think through them, if possible, to answers of your own. I take it for granted that the best if not the only solution will be a democratic one, which means that if we are to find it we must find it together. And since any claim I may make to special competence here rests only on method and not on content, you will do well to be wary. Your judgment of the facts, as well as of the way I arrange them and of any conclusions I may suggest as flowing from them, is now fully as good as mine.

We begin with two assumptions. One, to which the greater part of this book bears witness, is that an atomic and biological war is something to be avoided if possible; or, conversely, that stable peace in the world is a desirable objective. We shall have occasion to examine this assumption as we go along. The other, which I shall not undertake to substantiate at all, is that American-Soviet discord is the major force leading the world toward atomic and biological war; or, conversely, that the road to peace we are now exploring leads through improvement and stabilization of relations between our country and Russia.

But this latter assumption immediately raises our first question, which we shall attempt to deal with by exploring all the alternative answers to it.

Let us take the first question in this form: *Is accord with Russia possible for us?* Or, in other words, is there now any basis for a stable peace between the United States and the Soviet Union? The possible answers are "yes," "no," and "maybe."

For the answer "no," we had better look to antecedents as well as to consequences. In the United States many observers now offer a flat and unqualified "no" to this question. They are persuaded either that the Soviet Union or its rulers are so thoroughly corrupt as to be quite unworthy of even the minimal respect needed as a basis for accord or else that Russia is an imminent menace to our highest values, so that we can have no hope of security while she maintains her present structure. Some such premise can be found in our newspapers every day now, implied if not baldly stated. I have read and listened to many arguments for it, and I can say no more of them here than that I have not been convinced by them. To me the opinion is unsubstantiated; its roots appear to lie in emotion rather than in authenticated fact. It is currently popular and respectable in this country; indeed, any very sharp divergence from it is not only unpopular but may be dangerous. But we cannot let such a consideration color our inquiry. It is not essential for our purpose to prove that the opinion is in error, and I shall make no effort to do so. But, in view of its consequences, it does seem necessary to point out that it has not been proved to be true and that accordingly its alternatives may be worthy of exploration.

For the inevitable consequence of this answer, "no," is war. If accord is not possible, if there is no basis for a stable peace, then war must surely come. And if war is to come, the indications are that it would be less disastrous to have it come soon rather than to delay it. Time is on the side of the Russians. They suffered much more than we did from World War II and will recover their capacity to wage war increasingly as time goes on—at least so long as the prospect of war remains alive. And it is probable, of course, that in time they will have atomic bombs.

A seemingly logical conclusion to this line of thought is the so-called "preventive" war. A preventive American-Soviet war would presumably differ from one without the adjective in time, in the manner of its beginning, and in the weight of initial advantage. It would come sooner than the other kind. We would wage it deliberately. And we would hope that the combination of World-War-II damage to Russia and our atomic bombs would favor our cause decisively. A year or so ago there was talk of a "lightning" war, but nobody seems to credit this idea any more. It seems pretty well agreed by now that we could not hope to knock out the Russians all at once even if we could drop all the atomic bombs we have on them in one catastrophic blow. Their country is too big, their activities too widely spread. And at once their armies, poised on the borders of Europe and Asia, would overrun those continents and force us to carry the war there. Neither atomic bombs nor BW, as far as I know, have yet been taught to distinguish between friend and foe. Old-fashioned land fighting would ensue, and the war would be likely to drag on for several years. We would have started building a stockpile of undying hatred for ourselves among the peoples of the earth, who could not be counted upon to appreciate the purity of our motives. A delayed war might well be far worse than an immediate war; but the immediate war, however it started, would still be World War III in every important respect.

Preventive war is a snare, and war itself, as a solution to the problem of peace, is a delusion. None of which proves that "no" is the wrong answer to our question; but it encourages a look at the alternatives.

Suppose that the answer to our question (Is accord with Russia possible for us?) is a gloomy "maybe"—a grudging "yes, but only on our terms." Some such answer seems to be the basis for what the Russians call "atomic diplomacy." Our current foreign policy, indeed, seems to have in it an element of international poker, with loaded and cocked forty-fives on every hip, ours being loaded with atomic bullets. We gamble that threats, although they may bring us to within an inch of war, will not bring us to war because Russia is inherently weak and unable to fight. If only we get tough enough—so runs the argument—Russia must eventually capitulate, whereupon her leaders will be unseated and her structure changed so that we shall be able to deal with her. But we have tried increasing toughness for more than two years. As far as I can see the Russians are still holding on. True, it is difficult to interpret their behavior. If they are momentarily conciliatory it seems to be evidence of their weakness, meaning that our "get-tough" policy is having the desired effect, meaning that we need more of it. On the other hand if they refuse to budge we take it as evidence of their utter obstinacy, meaning that our "get-tough" policy is the only possible way to deal with them, meaning that we need more of it. Getting tough, whether it is done by a great nation or by the big boy on the block, can hope to succeed only if the victim is either a coward or a fool. Only history can show whether Russia is either of these or whether continued pressure can crack her structure as this kind of argument predicts. But any self-respecting boy or nation—we ourselves, for instance—would respond to toughness only by getting tougher.

But now suppose the answer to our question is "yes" or "maybe" with a spark of hope in it. Suppose we say, "yes (or maybe) accord with the Soviet Union is possible, even though she continues much as she is, without the changes that require violent upheaval." If we can answer our first question thus we can go on to the second one.

The second question, then, assumes that accord with Russia is possible as a basis for peace and asks: *What would be the cost of that peace?*

We cannot hope for a numerical answer to this question. Its terms are too many and too varied; not all of them are measurable, and some of them are not known. But we must do the best we can. One way of approaching an answer is to explore the elements that enter into estimates of the cost of war, on the one hand, and the cost of preventing war, on the other, in an effort to determine which is greater.

Some of the elements in the cost of World War II that were particularly difficult to appraise have been listed by Secretary of State Marshall as: "casualties among civilians; losses caused by the displacement of populations; 'the long-term effects of devoting the major portions of the world's over-all capabilities for a period of years to the objectives of destruction,' and the loss in the destruction of homes, industries, and means of livelihood of millions of people, which 'probably represented a greater monetary cost factor than the support of armed forces.'"

World War II was the last of the old-fashioned wars, in which, toward the end, only a corner of the curtain was raised on the war of today and tomorrow. Modern BW was not used, nor were guided missiles; jet propulsion was in its infancy, and only two atomic bombs fell, the total of their terrific destruction having been swallowed up in the statistics of the whole war. By November 21, 1945, according to information given out by the Vatican, there were 22,060,000 military and civilian dead and 34,400,000 wounded. These may be conservative figures, for two years later Secretary Marshall counted more than 15 million dead and missing *military* personnel alone, without including Poland and other smaller nations. Poland alone is said to have suffered about 6 million casualties, including both civilian and military, dead and wounded. But using the Vatican estimate, it is nevertheless apparent that in today's war a few hundred well-placed atomic bombs of the outmoded Hiroshima type might pile up an equal casualty list *in a single day!* There is no way of computing the number of casualties that might result from BW.

As for dollar costs, it has been estimated by official sources in Washington and by a survey made by the American University—with somewhat surprising precision—that the total military cost of World War II to all belligerents, excluding the eight-year war in China, was $1,116,991,463,084, with property damage of $230,900,000,000. That World War III would cost disproportionately more can hardly be doubted; but such dollar values alone can represent only a small fraction of the true total cost of war.

An illuminating editorial in the issue of *Business Week* for April 24, 1948, entitled "Economic Consequences of a Third World War," bears on some of the other kinds of cost that war would entail. I quote the two opening paragraphs:

"In a lot of ways, World War II was not hell for the U.S. Essentially, it was tragic. But there were some things—the elimination of unemployment, the general increases in incomes, the boom in business—that the country welcomed.

"But that wouldn't be true in a Third World War. Another war—if it should come—would be a grim and miserable business for everyone. There would be no compensations."

The article points out that between 1939 and 1944 we increased production by 75 per cent and were therefore able to pay for war while expanding both profits and wages, with higher prices and taxes taking away only part of these increases. But with output now near maximum, it could be still further increased to meet the demands of a new war only by longer hours and lower wages. In 1948, says *Business Week*, we were in the first stage of mobilization, with a 17-billion-dollar budget for armaments and European aid.* In the sec-

---

* President Truman's budget as presented to Congress on January 10, 1949, increased this figure to nearly 21 billion dollars. The figures as given in the *New York Herald Tribune* (January 11, 1949) are:

$14,267,500,779 for national defense
6,708,816,067 for international affairs and foreign aid

If to this total, $20,976,316,846, we add
5,495,529,254 for veterans' services and benefits
5,450,000,000 for interest on the public debt

the sum, $31,921,846,100, when compared with
the total budget, $41,858,000,000, shows that more than three-quarters of the cost of government is to be used to pay for war and the preparation for war.

ond stage government controls would be essential to sustain military production and at the same time prevent disastrous inflation. And with the onset of actual warfare, which the writers of this article feel sure would last for several years, "every corner of the economy would come under minute regulation from Washington." Materials controls would be much more extensive than they were in World War II. Controls over man power would be much more stringent, since, with unemployment gone and wages high, labor could not be enticed into war jobs but would have to be forced into them. Strikes would be flatly outlawed and incitement to strike treated as treason. "Civil rights of all kinds would take an awful beating, of course." Inflation would have to be held in check with drastic price ceilings, very high taxes, and forced savings; but even such measures might not be enough. In a long war the economy would come to operate under what these writers call "military communism."

I do not know just what "military communism" is. This picture seems to me strikingly similar to the industrial dictatorship geared to and sustained by war which, in an older day when certain words seemed clearer to us than they do now, we used to call "Fascism."

But emotionally colored words aside, this is one aspect of the cost of war as it is estimated by and for hardheaded businessmen. There would be inordinately high costs in human life, suffering, and dislocation, in damage to property and to the earth that feeds and sustains us all; but the highest cost might be in the very values for which the rest of the price was being paid—in the democracy that the war was being waged to preserve. According to the reasoning in this *Business Week* article we could not wage war without sacrificing the only purpose for which the war could be fought.

We ought to note at this point that the Russians, in their own peculiar way, are also hardheaded. They paid a much higher price for World War II than we did. Although they have been accused of underestimating the power of our atomic bombs, I think it unlikely that they are so innocent of knowledge about our power in general as to fail to appreciate how much a World War III would cost *them*.

Yet let us be on guard. High as the cost of war would undoubtedly be to us, is it not possible that the alternative cost—that of preventing war—would be equally high if not higher? Unfortunately this cost is even more difficult to measure.

It may be useful to approach this question of the cost of preventing war by recognizing that for most human beings, both in their private lives and in their collective activities, peace is *not* the highest value. Most of us, singly or in groups up to national dimensions, will fight if sufficiently provoked or if we believe that the prize to be fought for or to be saved by fighting is sufficiently precious. It is said of course to be a mark of advancing civilization that the individual learns increasingly to gain and preserve desirable ends without fighting; but this is not yet true of nations—although it may well be the goal toward which we aspire! The important point here, however, is that civilized or not most of us will fight if need be. We do not believe in peace at any price.

Accordingly the question of the cost of preventing war can be framed in terms of those values that we would fight in order to gain or preserve. And so the broader question can be broken down into smaller ones: What are the values? How precious are they? Can we preserve them without fighting? And could we be sure of preserving them if we fought?

Experience suggests to me that this is a section of the rocky road to peace that we will do best to traverse each in his own way. I can offer only a few hints. Whether and how you get over it depends heavily upon yourself. The ground is treacherous, beset for the unwary with semantic traps and emotional bogs, cluttered with the loose rocks and tangled vines of propaganda and counterpropaganda. You must test each step of the way with your own tread. You must evaluate for yourself such concepts as "political freedom" and "our competitive system" or whatever the values may be which you think we as a nation might fight for. You must endeavor to find out what these values are for you and to define them with the greatest possible precision, so that you can determine just how precious they are to you personally. If you are to contribute to a democratic decision on this great question you must do this job alone. It is of transcendent importance that you do it.

And having done it you may apply the results to the question of how best to preserve the values you have chosen. To what degree does American-Soviet discord endanger them? How much of this treasure, if any, would we have to sacrifice in order to maintain peace? And how much of it, if any, would we lose in war?

Or, in other words, which would cost more—war or the prevention of war? The line of reasoning I have outlined may bring you to a working answer to this question. But note. If you find that prevention would cost more than war, you are back to the "no" answer to the first question—war is the lesser evil. But if you find that war would cost more, then you may confront the third great question: *How shall we achieve peace?*

If you can reach this part of the road to peace you will have come through its roughest and most treacherous sections to comparatively open ground. What went before was the framework of the problem; what is left is the solution. Its achievement will certainly not be easy; but if enough of us can succeed in framing the problem satisfactorily the democratic solution we need should not be beyond our reach. Given a sufficient understanding of the issues, a well-informed public able to balance the great values at risk either must be able to win through to the sound objective toward which we strive, or else democracy is inherently weak and must fail. I think that most Americans will agree with me in believing that democracy is inherently strong. If so and if we all do our duty by it, we shall not fail.

I can find no better way to close this chapter than to indicate the position in which I find myself after having traveled over the same road. These are my own conclusions, and it should hardly be necessary to point out that you need not accept them. Perhaps my unavoidable bias has made them apparent in the gaps of my scientific objectivity; but there is no good reason why I should not state them frankly.

I came to the road, of course, by way of my experience with biological warfare, which persuaded me that the cost of World War III would be higher than most of us can imagine, and also via a critical contemporary observation of the road to failure through attempts at the international control of atomic energy. I had built no excessive hopes on these attempts and in consequence did not become unduly pessimistic when they failed. Likewise I watched the development of the Soviet Union with detachment through the eyes of an American newspaper reader with a scientific bent. It never seemed to me necessary to approach the subject of Russia with any great warmth either of affection or of aversion. I have found fascination in what seems to me to be a gigantic experiment in new social and political forms; and whether ultimately the experiment succeeds or fails I feel sure that we can learn important lessons from it if we wish to, just as, beyond doubt, the Russians can learn from us. But having built neither my hopes nor my fears upon the Soviet experiment it has been possible for me to watch its successes and its failures, its accomplishments and its transgressions—and there have of course been both—with neither vindictiveness nor disillusionment. I believe that the Soviet system is going to remain in the world for a while, although doubtless it will be modified as time passes. And today it seems to me that the so-called "menace" of Soviet Communism is vastly overrated. If the United States is really strong—as I believe it is—and if our strength resides, not in military power and aggressiveness, but in the character and the way of life of our people—as I believe it does—then I am sure we have nothing to fear from the Russians or from any other nation. Moreover I believe that both the Russian people and their leaders want a durable peace, if only because they, too, must realize what a World War III would cost them. I think it likely that, if they were given half a chance, they would help find and willingly accept reasonable means toward peace. Accordingly there seems to me to be no real doubt that accord with Russia is possible for us. My answer to our first question is an emphatic "yes."

I believe also that the cost of preventing an American-Soviet war would not only be less than the cost of war itself but that, if purchased with due regard to the values as I see them, this cost of peace would be much lower than the price of any other commodity now for sale in the market of international politics. Not only would the cost of war be appallingly high; it seems unavoidable to me that we can only lose our American heritage—however differently you and I may define that term—in any attempt to secure it through war or even through extended preparation for war. Nearly all our current difficulties appear to be intimately related to our fear that an American-Soviet war is inevitable. From our vast budget for armaments to hysteria over spies, from the high cost of living to the uncomfortable need we feel to support any nation anywhere that may join us in opposing Russia, whether it be democratic, feudal, or Fascist—so long as it is not communist—all these disturbing circumstances are interlocked with fear of war, fear that impels us blindly and unthinkingly toward destruction. If we could but have the courage of our convictions and come to exert upon the world the strength of a great nation at peace we might solve most of our problems by solving the central one and save the greatest part of the price into the bargain.

War is not inevitable and cannot be desirable. We are the strongest nation on earth and the richest. We suffered least among the larger belligerents from World War II. We made the atomic bomb and used it, and we have worked and are now working to develop BW and other weapons of the new war. I believe that we have made mistakes, but so have all nations, like all individuals. We need feel no national guilt, and we need have no fear. Given only a sound belief in our own true strength we could afford to be generous in our approach to other nations, including Russia. If we could approach the international conference table with the respect for others that would grow out of true faith in ourselves we might find a solution to the problem of peace that all of us could accept. I do not think we have tried this yet, and I know of no experiment that promises so much.

13. GOOD, BAD, AND WORSE

SCIENCE is a tool with which problems may be explored and layed open for solution. It is most effective in dealing with problems whose elements can be weighed or measured or at least isolated; but as it continues to be applied with successful results the horizon of its usefulness expands increasingly. It has explored the perceptible world inward toward the ultimate structure of matter and energy and outward through the galaxies of infinite space; it is closing its grip on the molecular patterns of life and breaking through the barriers that hide the laws of behavior, both individual and social. But wherever it goes it finds certain questions in its path with which thus far it cannot deal at all and which, if it is to move on, it can only by-pass or ignore—questions of good and bad, of right and wrong, which are neither less real nor less significant to us because of our inability to measure them and therefore to agree upon them. There are questions of this kind in biological warfare; and having traversed those areas of the subject with which science can deal more or less confidently and come through an effort to apply science to the much less tractable fields of politics, we now emerge upon territory in which science is of no use to us at all. Here, if we are to make any progress, we will do best to hang the cloak of science outside and venture in simply as human beings.

The kinds of question with which I now propose to deal,

without scientific pretensions, are these: Is biological warfare "horrible"? Is it "worse" than other kinds of war? And is it "good" or "bad" for human beings to participate in it? I shall bring to bear on these questions such facts and as much clear reasoning as I can muster; but their true basis is emotional, and my conclusions will be no more than one man's opinion.

By way of introduction to this general subject let us consider an ethical idea which serves, I think, as a tacit foundation for all science. It is the belief that man is the "best," the "most important" of all things living and nonliving, that he is the highest value, and that all other values are arranged in relation to him. Stated or unstated, I think science must have as its ultimate purpose to improve the lot of man. That the individual scientist frequently either fails to acknowledge or consciously repudiates this idea does not invalidate it; and we might find, if we knew how to look, that the scientist who rejects it is in the measure of his rejection an ineffective scientist. I am attempting to suggest not that scientists *ought to* believe in the priority of man but that unless they do they cannot proceed successfully or seriously to frame problems and to solve them. The fruits of this idea can be the primary reward of scientific work—a sense of personal importance or fulfillment which everyone must find somewhere if he is to be sustained through life. But with the scientist as with the artist—and in this respect the two are akin—the source of fulfillment may be so rich that all other sources are subordinated to it. Accordingly its value is often translated into dollars by the canny employers of scientists and duly deducted from their pay checks.

I am not by any means implying that the scientist is in any general sense more moral than other men: I know too many obvious examples to the contrary. He ranges in his religion from supreme orthodoxy to utter unbelief, and in his daily life outside the laboratory from saint to scoundrel. So long as he stays out of jail and the grave these attributes need not affect his conduct as a scientist; but I suggest that either he preserves his integrity in the laboratory, or he is not a scientist. And the special integrity of the scientist can, I think, be reduced as its essence to a belief in the supreme value of mankind, with science as its helpful servant.

This idea of the supremacy of man as a dominating principle is of course not peculiar to science. Indeed it seems to be basic to most human cultures and religions, with some possibly significant exceptions, such as Nazi Germany and imperial Japan. In our own culture it is a paramount principle of law; and again it may be significant that only the duly constituted authorities of government can defy it with impunity in the punishment of crime or in war. But this byway leads out of our field of inquiry, and we shall pursue it no further.

It is the concept of man as the highest value that makes practically impossible, as I suggested in Chap. 6, the use of unwilling human subjects for scientific experiments. I say "unwilling" because obviously human volunteers can be and frequently are used in this way. Often they are the scientists themselves, but if there is any risk to the subject in the experiment, the human guinea pigs must have come to appreciate the risk, to balance it against the reward, and to decide that the undertaking is worth while. I have mentioned the instance of the Nazis whose human experiments were an expression of their general depravity. It seems to me to be axiomatic that these experiments could not have been planned or carried out by scientists and that they necessarily failed to yield useful results. (And, incidentally, I find a clear indication of the fundamental dissimilarity of Hitler's Germany and Stalin's Russia in the low estate to which science fell in the former country, despite its earlier preeminence, and the flourishing state of science in the Soviet Union.)

One can clearly discern the dominance of this idea of the primacy of human life in experimentation with animals. It is the justification of such experimentation that it yields knowledge bearing directly or indirectly upon human problems, implying that human values are necessarily higher than those of the "lower" animals. The scientist who works with animals never quite loses sight of the essentially moral purpose of the experiment. He does not "vivisect" animals out of hatred or contempt for them, such as the Nazis had for Poles and Jews. Indeed he cannot hate them or hold them in contempt and still use them effectively. Frequently, and especially if he has worked for any great length of time with any given animal or single species, he develops a considerable attachment for them. This does not prevent his handling them effectively to suit his scientific objective so long as he keeps in mind the purpose of his work in terms of its value to man. A laboratory worker who abused animals or was in any real sense cruel in his handling of them would at once be recognized by his fellow workers as lacking in the essential qualities of a scientist.

Experiments that come closer to breaking the human-supremacy rule than any others I know of but which were nevertheless of very real value have been conducted to test a vaccine and the sulfa drugs in preventing or curing plague. These were "controlled" experiments, in which alternate subjects were left unvaccinated or untreated. The vaccine studies were performed in Java with a *living* but attenuated plague culture, and the drug experiments came from India. It is remarkable that they are among the very few controlled human experiments with highly fatal diseases to be found in the scientific record. We frequently complain about the lack of such experiments and of the resulting difficulty in deciding just how useful a vaccine or a drug may be.

There seem to have been extenuating circumstances in both the Javanese and the Indian experiments. Although the human subjects presumably had no choice as to their status in either study as experimental guinea pigs or controls, they were certainly not the kind of unwilling victims that the Nazis used. The experimental manipulations in both were of course intended to be directly helpful rather than harmful. It may be a partial justification of the vaccine experiment that it had to be conducted on a limited group of subjects and that outside the group others in plague areas were necessarily as unprotected as the controls. In the Indian experiments there seems to have been a parallel justification in a shortage of sulfa drugs, which made it inevitable that some subjects would go untreated. Indeed, some of the deaths among treated subjects were attributed to insufficient drug. Nevertheless, there is testimony to the importance of the principle of man as the highest value in the fact that very few scientists attempt such experiments and that their spines tingle when they read the record of one. You may recall that Sinclair Lewis's Dr. Arrowsmith flunked Dr. Gottlieb's crucial test on this very question, thereby, perhaps, proving himself a man rather than a cold-blooded scientist. It is my contention, of course, that the blood of scientists has the same temperature as yours.

The idea of human supremacy may be nearest the surface in biological science because of the inescapable kinship of man with the whole biological world; but whether it is clearly appreciated or not I think it pervades and dominates all science. The wholehearted postwar effort of atomic scientists to divert their bomb away from destruction and toward human betterment has been a highly moral performance which I can interpret not as a conversion but at most as an awakening; the idea of man as the dominant value must have been in their minds even while they were developing and perfecting the bomb. Yet there seems to be a paradox here. How can science aimed at the destruction of human life still cherish the notion that human life is the highest value?

An attempt to resolve this paradox by reason alone could in my judgment end only in absurdity. Yet the scientist who devotes his efforts to war research must resolve it if he is not to lose his identity as a scientist, whether he does so clearly and vigorously or more obscurely; but the resolution must have an intrinsic emotional component which science does not yet know how to define. The conflict must be resolved, I think, positively and not negatively. The compelling motive must be the protection of friends and loved ones rather than the destruction of enemies; yet it cannot be simple self-preservation alone, personal or social. There must be in it as well some larger concept of human welfare, a belief, however incompletely realized, that the future of all men demands a transient lapse into the antiscientific business of human destruction. In time of war or if the danger of war is clear and imminent, most scientists, like other men, find no great difficulty in resolving the conflict in their own minds sufficiently to direct a course of action which we cover and condone under the wartime meaning of the word "patriotism." Certainly this happened in World War II, when scientists in unprecedented numbers entered voluntarily and enthusiastically into our war effort, developed and perfected the most destructive weapons and yet never lost their identity as scientists. In my opinion this course of action was compelled by circumstances for a preponderantly social purpose; it was unavoidable, and therefore it was good. Any guilt feelings that may now remain in the minds of individual scientists must therefore betray an incomplete resolution of the conflict rather than any inherent defect in the principle upon which the action was based.

A corollary of this proposition needs only brief mention for the present—that since war distorts or inverts so many normal values, what is true in war may not be true in peace. The meaning of the word "patriotism" is an example. To achieve its full intensity this word must have a glandular component; in peacetime nearly everybody can find at least some significance in Samuel Johnson's definition of it as "the last refuge of a scoundrel."

One of the secondary elements in the conflict which the scientist must resolve before he can lend his special talents to war is the *kind* of human destruction involved. For obscure reasons this seems to make a difference. There are various ways of destroying men, and while all of them are morally bad, some seem worse than others. Which brings us to a consideration of BW as the "worst" or "most horrible" of weapons.

Some very responsible men have expressed this idea publicly. James F. Byrnes, for example, when he was Secretary of State, considered BW, compared with the atomic bomb, "an even more frightful method of human destruction"; and Walter Lippmann, prompted by the United States Navy release of January 4, 1946, regarded BW as "even more deadly and malignant" than the bomb. Similar thoughts have been expressed by many others; and, indeed, the notion was prevalent even during the war that there is something peculiarly repugnant or unclean about BW that does not apply to the atomic bomb or to other weapons. I am assuming that this is predominantly an emotional rather than a purely rational reaction; at all events I see no way of dealing with it at the level of reason alone. A man can be no deader than dead, nor can his death or suffering be more lingering or painful, so far as I can imagine, than death or suffering inflicted by atomic energy toward the fringe of its immediate effects or by an injury from high explosive which leads to death slowly through prolonged suffering. Possibly there is an element in this judgment of the perversion of cherished good into evil; of the sciences of disease, so traditionally bent immediately toward the alleviation of human suffering, being turned deliberately upside down. We shall come back to this idea later in another form. It seems to me to be excuse rather than explanation; the question may be one of taste and no more arguable than varying human preferences for clothing, music, or cheese. It goes almost without saying that the military will have none of such quibbling; in this instance I find myself in agreement with them.

But there may also be a rational component in the judgment that BW is "worse" than the atomic bomb. Secretary Byrnes presumably had competent technical guidance behind his statement, while Mr. Lippmann's terms may have more specific meanings than the word "frightful"; he may have implied that BW is capable of killing larger numbers of victims than the atomic bomb. Is BW "worse" than the atomic bomb in this more restricted sense? I frankly do not know. It is impossible to make quantitative comparisons, for whereas we have abundant and precise information on the destructiveness of the atomic bomb, we have nothing of the kind for BW because it has not been used in war. Yet there are some comparisons that can be made.

It must be clear from what I have said in earlier chapters that BW is in many respects very different from atomic warfare, although there are a few striking similarities as well. We have already compared the ways in which they lend themselves to technical schemes for international control and found them very dissimilar. Here we are concerned with them as weapons, and especially with their destructiveness.

The atomic bomb, within the range of its greatest blast and thermal effects, is both instantaneous and indiscriminate in its destructive results; neither life of any kind nor anything physically breakable or burnable escapes. BW, on the other hand, would have both a selective and a delayed action. It would have little or no influence on property; its targets would be only certain particular kinds of living things; and the resulting damage would be manifested only after a lag corresponding with the incubation period of the agent. On the other hand radiation injuries produced beyond the blast zone of the bomb or behind partial shielding resemble those of BW: they also have a lag and range in final consequences from death through extended suffering to recovery with or without permanent damage; and they include at least the possibility of extremely protracted injury. Although both can be used in different ways the atomic bomb is a single kind of weapon, whereas BW is many different weapons. The results of an atomic bombing would be comparatively uniform both in kind and in extent, and the military applications of the bomb are therefore narrowly limited. BW, on the contrary, is extremely flexible and could be employed to yield a wide range of different effects, from a high concentration of casualties, either localized or spreading, to subtle or insidious disruption of normal activity induced psychologically rather than physically.

If we exclude the lesser kinds of BW sabotage, both are terror weapons applicable only to all-out war. Neither offers any encouraging prospects for defense.

BW is probably very much cheaper in terms of destruction to be expected per unit of cost or per unit of munition weight. I do not know which is capable of producing greater over-all damage; but BW has one dubious advantage to the intended victim. In comparable positions in relation to the center of atomic-bomb or BW attacks, you might have no chance whatever of escaping death from the bomb but a very good chance of escaping death from the germs. Let us also bear in mind that whereas atomic bombs are effective beyond any doubt, there is a lingering doubt on this score for BW that cannot be resolved unless it is used in war.

Which is worse? You will either have to decide for yourself or join me in uncertainty. I have seen the curious phenomenon repeated of physicists who think BW is likely to be worse and of biologists who feel sure that the atomic bomb is worse. Maybe familiarity breeds a little contempt, or fear of the unknown tips the balance. But it must be an emotion of some kind rather than cold fact.

Moral judgments regarding distinctively "evil" weapons of war are, of course, an old story, and the history of the world's efforts to codify them goes back a long way. It is on the whole a futile history, for there is no reason to believe that international agreements outlawing particular weapons have ever had the slightest effect. Today few people seem to place any stock in them, although Mr. Gromyko has continued somewhat plaintively to suggest that what the world now needs above all else is a good convention outlawing bad weapons.

Back in the thirteenth century the Council of Lateran declared the cross bow illegal in war, and a couple of hundred years later Bayard demanded that the musket be outlawed as a coward's weapon which could be used to kill a brave knight without engaging him in combat. How true! Even then the sport of kings had begun to deteriorate. Yet it did not seem to be the game itself that was at fault but only the rules that needed amending to match the complications continually and awkwardly introduced by progress.

We have had what seem to me to be quite similar moral judgments in recent times. Indeed as recently as July, 1947, the Fourth International Congress of Microbiology at Copenhagen, in a resolution against BW whose intent is wholly laudable, found it necessary to describe this form of warfare as "barbaric" and "absolutely unworthy of any civilized community." A week earlier, at Stockholm, the International

Cytological Congress had also passed a resolution on BW, but in this instance no moral judgment was offered. This group of scientists stated that "we as biologists are especially concerned with the prevention of all warfare, and in particular of biological warfare." They also resolved to "set up a committee to offer technical advice and assistance to the United Nations . . . on this problem"; but nothing has come of the resolution to my knowledge.

Before World War I, the Hague Convention outlawed "poison or poisoned arms" and stated that the right of belligerents in war is not unlimited, that war must not be used for the purpose of inflicting unnecessary injuries or for the wanton devastation and spoliation of enemy property, and that war must not be waged against the peaceful inhabitants of the enemy territory. After Guernica, Rotterdam, Coventry, Lidice, Berlin, and Hiroshima these pious sentiments ring quaintly on our ears. How old-fashioned the ancients were! But although none of the belligerents in World War I were restrained by these injunctions, and after the Germans had introduced poison-gas warfare, the Washington Disarmament Conference of 1922 reaffirmed the prohibitions of the Hague Convention and extending that on poisons to include all "asphyxiating gases and all analogous liquids, materials, or devices." And the last great convention, the Geneva Protocol, signed on June 17, 1925, prohibited not only poisonous and asphyxiating gases but also, specifically, bacteriological warfare. This pact was signed at the time by the United States and was ultimately ratified by forty-one nations, including France, England, the Soviet Union, and Germany. It was never ratified, however, either by Japan or by the United States. On April 8, 1946, President Truman withdrew it from the Senate along with eighteen other unratified treaties. The world had just come through the greatest, most destructive, and therefore doubtless the most immoral war of all history, in which neither side had shown any clearly visible hesitation in the development and use of new weapons. It is true that neither chemical warfare nor biological warfare was used—the latter, at all events, not by any of the United Nations—and this fact has encouraged both Russian and American spokesmen to insist that each nation had abided by the pledges of the Geneva Protocol. But the two kinds of warfare had been developed with considerable enthusiasm by both sides in World War II, and there is neither direct evidence that I know of nor indirect evidence in the form of obvious moral scruple in the use of other weapons that lends the slightest credence to the idea that they were withheld for ethical reasons. The reasons, I do not doubt, were strictly military, or what I have elsewhere described as "realistic."

Nowadays few of us retain any faith in the usefulness of treaties outlawing weapons. But let us pause to recognize that there are at least two rather different ways of looking at this idea. The distinction between these two ways of regarding international conventions seems to me vitally important.

It is one thing to argue that treaties outlawing the use of weapons in war, weapons of any sort, are in themselves useless; but it is quite another matter to insist that international treaties of any kind are mere scraps of paper unless they are backed up by force. There is no reason to believe that the international prohibition of weapons has ever been effective. There are also plenty of examples of infraction or utter disregard of treaties of other kinds, particularly during the period of the rise of Fascism in the 1930's. But these more general treaties, unlike the others, and even though they were not implemented by force, have not been broken *universally*. The whole United Nations and its many highly successful agencies —which are too often submerged by those that have failed—

bear living testimony to the world's confidence in and reliance on treaties.

Having passed through a period of increasing international anarchy which culminated in the most ruthless of all wars, many of us seem to have become excessively cynical. We have come to believe that international agreement is impossible and that only force can save us. But that a stable peace cannot be achieved through the use of force seems to me a truism. Either we must have international agreements of some kind, arrived at through peaceful negotiation and based on mutual respect and confidence among nations rather than on force, or else peace lies forever beyond our reach. If we are to have any hope of peace, we must *begin* with treaties. Even a treaty outlawing weapons might be a good thing to begin with if it could be recognized as no more than a starting point. We must assume that treaties have been broken not necessarily because they were in themselves faulty but because the international climate in which they grew could not nourish a healthy plant. It is the climate and not the fruit that needs to be changed.

And likewise it is not weapons but war that must be eliminated. So long as war is permitted to happen it will inevitably be as ruthless as the times and their knowledge and power can make it. Moral distinctions among weapons are meaningless, and in my opinion to single out BW—or any other weapon or kind of warfare—as particularly "horrible" or ethically "worse" can find neither useful purpose nor justification. All war is horrible.

Which, by a circular path, brings us to the physician. In proportion as BW impinges upon the field of medicine it may tread on some of the most sensitive ethical toes to be found in any shoe. For to the doctor the principle that human life is the highest value is not arguable; it is the keystone of his openly avowed ethics. He is dedicated to the alleviation of human suffering, to the prevention and cure of disease; he cannot under any circumstances participate in the destruction of human life. Or so it would seem.

Some of my best friends are physicians. I have often discussed this delicate question with them—including some who were my colleagues in BW research—and most of them agree that the ablest physicians are those who make the fewest pretensions, or none at all, to special status in the human family. A physician is a human being, and when he follows the thread of his own principle through to its logical conclusion he finds that he is not "better" than other human beings for the simple and compelling reason that there can be nothing better: man is the highest value. It therefore follows, in this instance inexorably, that what is good for other men is also good for physicians.

If it is right for a scientist to engage in war research whose purpose is the destruction of human life, it is equally right for a physician to do so. I have not proved and cannot prove that it is right for either; I only affirm that it is, given the real and imminent danger that makes the act necessary and therefore good. The inhabitants of the city of Frederick during the war knew from the high concentration of medical tags on Camp Detrick car license plates that there were many physicians there. The best of them participated in the work of the camp with an enthusiasm that could not have been surpassed by that of any physicist at Oak Ridge or Los Alamos. They had resolved their personal conflict with equal clarity and vigor. There was little reluctance to be seen among them; and when it appeared this feeling seemed to be a manifestation of squeamishness or confusion rather than of courage or perspicacity. In my judgment it was the physicians who participated wholeheartedly in BW rather than those who knowingly hung back who reflected the more credit upon their great profession.

But scientist and physician alike, as I have suggested, could lend their special talents to the destruction of man only in the hope that by so doing they were serving the larger purpose of more general human preservation. To most of us at Camp Detrick during World War II this was a sound position. But what of a World War III, in which the cost of war will have mounted so high as to make any true victory for either side seem unattainable? If it should seem likely or even possible that we might have to destroy more men than we could hope to save and in addition that the humanitarian values that seemed to justify the war could only be lost by fighting, how then would the paradox be resolved?

We can be reasonably sure of one thing. If World War III is allowed to come, biologists and men of all related fields, including physicians, will be called upon as never before to serve alongside physicists and other scientists as instruments of human destruction. I don't know how they will manage to do so and still retain their integrity. Indeed, I can't answer the question I have raised, and I suspect that it has no answer. It is a fragment of the larger question toward which this whole book is directed. Perhaps there are no fragmentary answers but only one: *Let us have peace.*

14. ON THE POSITIVE SIDE

Follow Seventh Street west for a mile and a half out of sedate little Frederick, Maryland, where Barbara Fritchie defied the rebels, and you will come upon the barracks, the yellow-tile laboratory and plant buildings and the tall brick chimneys of Camp Detrick. Before 1943 this space was an open airfield. Now it is a headquarters of the United States Army Chemical Corps, small as army camps go but one of the biggest and best-equipped installations in the world for biological research and development. Here, during World War II, a few hundred scientists and their helpers worked to make weapons out of germs and hammer out armor against them. And now, in the uneasy peace, through inertia, fear, and maybe little dreams of power, the same job goes on.

There is something wrong with this picture. 1943 was a critical year for us; things were not going very well. The Germans reached Stalingrad; we tasted victory in North Africa and drenched Salerno with American blood; Normandy was a year away. In the Pacific, too, Japan had reached her crest. We had won back Guadalcanal and were fighting bitterly for New Guinea; "island hopping" was just beginning, and Japan itself had felt no bombs but Doolittle's. The danger of BW loomed large to those who thought of it, and the need for Camp Detrick was real and pressing. It was built with as patriotic a fervor as possessed any infantry platoon or air squadron or tank factory; and scientists shared the fervor like other men. The war was young, and its outcome was far from sure; Camp Detrick was necessary, and therefore it was good. This is the simple logic of war; and no scientist who is also a man need feel anything but pride that he was driven by it.

But times have changed, and our values have changed with them. Having won the bloodiest war in all history, two great nations, each slightly swollen with pride, seem to be striving to divide the world between them; and in both men prepare for another and even bloodier war. In 1943 war was real and danger imminent; few failed to be touched by it and to participate willingly in it. Now war is cold in more than one sense. Nobody wants it openly. To many the threat of a new conflict seems to have a fabricated quality, like that of a fight between the local bully and the new boy. Suspended between fear of war and hope of peace, while grasping neither, we prepare wearily for the one while we yearn desperately for the other. And in this mood the need for BW seems less clear, its logic less compelling. What was once necessary has become doubtful, so that the smell of evil hangs over it inexorably. The smoke that now rises from the chimneys of Camp Detrick is symbolic of the great dilemma of our time.

What might be done with Camp Detrick and with its sister installations for BW, wherever they may exist in other countries, if we had peace? If we could dissolve the doubt of our times in a stable peace and, with the true values of peace, if we could come to recognize BW as an unmitigated evil, could we nevertheless find any good in what was built for it and done by it? Does BW have a positive side? Indeed it does.

About one hundred fifty technical papers and monographs published from Camp Detrick since January, 1946, testify to the positive contributions to peaceful science made by its staff during World War II and since. Yet these were by-products of BW research and development, published under a liberal policy that released everything of practical or fundamental scientific value in a constructive sense but nothing else. Nobody pretends that this work justified the cost of building Camp Detrick or that this alone could persuade our Congress to pass its current appropriations. But it is remarkable that so much good—good by stable peacetime standards—has come out of BW; and the fact testifies to the vastly greater volume of good that might come out of the resources of BW if only stable peace could be a reality.

I shall demonstrate a valid point here, but let me not overemphasize it. For both the good and the evil that may come of science, atomic energy is now our yardstick. We have already compared BW with the atomic bomb as a weapon of war. On the positive side it must be admitted without quibbling that there is nothing in the prospect of BW reconverted to peace, so far as I can see, that can compare in magnitude with the promise of atomic power. Yet, orders of magnitude aside, we need not doubt that the world would profit from BW far more in peace than in war, just as it would from atomic energy. In fact, I have no doubt that the peacetime value of BW, including not only its plant and facilities but, curiously enough, its topsy-turvy philosophy as well, would more than justify its total cost.

I have referred to many of the published reports from Camp Detrick, but more to point out their significance to BW than to stress their value as healthy science. We were standing on our heads at the time. But it was as healthy science that they were published; and it is necessary to set the record straight by looking at these papers and some others now that our feet are back on the ground and our heads are upright.

It seems hardly necessary to speak again of 2,4-D and the

other synthetic plant-growth regulators. You know their value as weed killers, and if by chance you are a sufferer from ragweed hay fever you may even feel that 2,4-D alone justifies the whole cost of BW. But these substances have many other uses, not all of which have yet been realized. Properly applied they can speed up the growth of plants instead of destroying them. They can prevent the germination of seeds and enable us to grow seedless fruits, tomatoes, or melons. Through the control of crop development they may help to overcome the ravages of uncontrolled agriculture which has contributed to the formation of dust bowls and deserts. And as tools in basic studies of growth and particularly in studies of the nucleus which dominates the activities of the living cell, they may play their part in uncovering the inner secrets of life itself. A practical by-product of this sort of research is increased understanding of those aberrant cell growths we call "cancer." The positive side of the Camp Detrick studies on plant-growth regulators, in which nearly eleven hundred different compounds were tested and their properties described, clearly outweighs the negative.

The crystallization of botulinus toxin, an accomplishment which we made the starting point for a detour into doubtful arithmetic, is also of much greater value as a contribution to sound knowledge than to BW. A series of papers on different phases of this subject have appeared from Camp Detrick. In addition to the independent studies of the Lamanna and Abrams groups on the crystallization of type A toxin itself, there have been other reports by Lamanna and his collaborators giving many properties of the type A toxin and reporting the isolation of type B toxin. Both toxins belong in that category of highly complex nitrogen-containing compounds called "proteins," among which are found the principal components of cell-substance or protoplasm. The type A toxin has a very large molecule, from 450,000 to

550,000 times as large as the molecule of hydrogen. The molecule of the type B toxin seems to be very much smaller. The type A toxin has been more extensively examined thus far, but it is clear that it differs markedly from the other, despite the fact that the two have essentially identical poisonous effects. It is curious that analysis of the type A toxin has revealed nothing that distinguishes this protein from those found generally in cell substance—nothing, in other words, that explains its extraordinarily poisonous nature. The fascinating suggestion has also been made for type A toxin that, notwithstanding its huge molecule and its tiny fatal dose (both adjectives are relative) there may be more than 20 million molecules packed into a single 50 per cent infective dose for the white mouse!

These studies of botulinus toxin are an important scientific achievement. The scientists who brought them to a successful conclusion merit the honor of having been the first to crystallize a bacterial toxin. Since their work was done at Camp Detrick under secrecy regulations obtaining during the war, its publication was delayed; and a paper by others on similar findings with tetanus toxin appeared immediately following the report of the Lamanna group in *Science* for May 17, 1946. Earlier work with diphtheria toxin and more recent experiments with other bacterial toxins have brought forth highly but still incompletely purified products. The isolation of botulinus and tetanus toxins as pure substances should spur final isolation of the others and their availability put in the hands of the chemist powerful tools for exploring some of the basic problems of disease. As with other fundamental scientific discoveries one cannot predict just what this one will lead to, but, assuming only peaceful scientific progress, we may be confident that its results will be of great value.

A broad group of researches with important results, undertaken both at Camp Detrick and at other laboratories under the BW program, were those devoted to the development of new or improved vaccines for protection against specific infections. Some of these were made in the veterinary field, resulting in the production of effective vaccines against two major diseases of poultry and one of cattle. The work on the two poultry infections, Newcastle disease and fowl plague, was done at Harvard University. Here existing laboratories were remodeled, so as to prevent escape of the viruses to neighboring Massachusetts farms, using safety precautions similar to those previously mentioned as essential to all work with highly infective agents. Careful study of these viruses then yielded, in addition to effective vaccines for both, improved methods for their prompt recognition and a considerable increase in knowledge of the natural manner of spread of the diseases which will be useful in controlling them.

Of equal or even greater importance is the development of a potent vaccine against rinderpest, a highly contagious cattle disease found in many parts of the world although not in North America. Because it is absent from this part of the world and if introduced might have had disastrous consequences for American cattle, the work with rinderpest virus was not only surrounded with the usual elaborate safety precautions but in addition was hidden away on an island in the St. Lawrence River, Grosse Ile. Here a joint American-Canadian group was headed under the BW program by Dr. Richard Shope, the veterinary virus specialist well known for his basic studies of swine influenza. An unusual "Note" preceding the extensive reports of this work is worth quoting at some length:

"The purpose of the project was to develop ways and means of protecting the livestock industry of the North American continent against a foreign plague that might be introduced intentionally, as an enemy method of 'biological warfare,' or accidentally.

"Six officers of the United States Army Veterinary Corps, one from the Medical Corps of the United States Navy, and two Canadian scientists, together with a corps of technicians from both countries, were assigned to the project. The highly successful outcome of the work in developing protective measures against rinderpest, one of the most devastating diseases of cattle, including improved methods of vaccine production plus fundamental observations significant to virus-disease research constitute an outstanding contribution to veterinary science and another shining example of what can be accomplished through collaboration of scientists from several fields."

Several investigations aimed at the production of immunizing agents were carried on at Camp Detrick itself. Some of these had immediately practical results, while others yielded information of fundamental scientific interest, promising future advances in our understanding of the process of infection. Part of the program of work with botulinus toxins included the development of harmless immunizing preparations, or toxoids, which were used successfully to protect workers at Camp Detrick against botulism just as other toxoids protect against diphtheria and tetanus. While there were no cases of botulism reported from Camp Detrick, it is uncertain just how much credit for this good record can be given to the toxoid injections. The injections were given not as a "human experiment" but to protect everyone who might need protection. The proved value of this procedure for experimental animals, however, and analogy with the excellent protection provided by toxoids in other diseases suggest that botulinus toxoids belong where we have put them provisionally in an earlier chapter—in the small group of "best" vaccines for diseases of man.

Psittacosis is another disease for which a vaccine was developed sufficiently at Camp Detrick for use in man. Its application to immunize those at Camp Detrick who handled this agent was justified by the fact that it contained no living virus and was harmless and by encouraging results in the protection of experimental animals with it. But since there were again no experiments with human subjects—none of those who handled the virus were left unvaccinated—it is impossible to say just how good the vaccine may be. In the one case of infection with this virus reported from the camp the patient had been successfully vaccinated; and while the vaccine may have prevented him from being more seriously ill, it obviously did not protect him against infection.

Experiments aimed at development of a completely safe vaccine against anthrax fell short of achieving their final purpose during the war but yielded information of considerable fundamental interest. There had already been several kinds of anthrax vaccines for use in animals but none suitable for use in man. One of the animal vaccines was the preparation of weakened but not killed anthrax germs made famous by Pasteur in his dramatic public experiments at Pouilly-le-Fort in France in 1881; this and several others were effective but not entirely safe and were therefore not suitable for use in man, while safe vaccines were of doubtful protective value. At Camp Detrick an intensive effort was made to apply new chemical techniques toward the development of a vaccine that would have both properties—complete safety and effectiveness—so that it could be used in man as well as in cattle and other animals in which anthrax is a serious economic problem.

This study stemmed from initial observations of a marked difference in natural resistance to anthrax in one group of experimental animal species as compared with another. The rabbit, for instance, succumbs much more easily than the white rat. Correlated with this difference were changes in appearance of diseased cells and tissues under the microscope which suggested that protective substances as well as destructive ones might be present there. Chemical methods were applied, and with their aid two substances were obtained in germfree extracts from infected skin taken from rabbits. One of these substances, the anthrax "inflammatory factor," when injected back into rabbits by itself—that is, without any living anthrax bacilli—reproduced a sort of damage much like that caused by the living virulent germs. This substance was partly purified, and its origin was traced to the outer layer, or capsule, of the anthrax bacillus. Its effect seems to be similar in kind to that of capsular substances of other disease-producing germs—like the pneumococcus, whose capsular starch is known to constitute the secret of its virulence.

The other substance turned up in this anthrax research had distinct protective value and was used, again in germfree extracts, to immunize animals against many fatal doses of living anthrax bacilli. This substance seems to come not from the germ itself but from the products of infection—from the chemical battleground of germs and animal substance—and is evidently a factor in the animal's natural resistance and ability to recover from the disease. Unfortunately the substance is very unstable, and attempts to purify it were not successful. If it can be obtained in sufficient amount, in stable form, and adequately free from animal-tissue components, it should provide a much more effective vaccine against the disease than any used up to this time.

Among many other individual contributions from the Camp Detrick laboratories, in a list too long for recounting here, some of the positive advances that were drawn from the accidental laboratory infections ought to be mentioned. I have spoken repeatedly of these infections in their important relationships to BW itself. They resulted because, at the time the camp was built, nobody knew how to prevent such accidents in work with highly infective agents. During the course of the war these very experiences and others at the camp taught us how prevention could be accomplished. In addition the cases of illness provided material for successful tests on the use of new remedies.

Among the newer antibiotic drugs, streptomycin, which has since become well established, was then new and experimental. Trials with it at Camp Detrick helped to make its value clear. Animal experiments with this and other remedies had been carried out at the camp and made it possible to select the most likely drug for treatment of human cases of illness as they appeared. Since there was usually a direct clue to diagnosis, which might otherwise have been difficult, in the circumstance that the patient had been working with one of the highly infective agents studied at the camp, it was possible to start treatment early and generally to give it under favorable circumstances. As a result cases of glanders were treated effectively with sulfadiazine, anthrax with penicillin, and tularemia with streptomycin. The one reported case of psittacosis was treated successfully with a combination of penicillin and sulfadiazine. This combination was used because the patient had been working with several agents and because treatment was started before the diagnosis of psittacosis could be confirmed by isolation of the virus from his sputum. There were in addition at least seventeen severe cases of brucellosis. All recovered, but in spite of rather than because of treatment with any of the individual drugs tried. This experience showed, probably more clearly than any other, that sulfa drugs and the antibiotics then available were of little value in treating brucellosis when used individually; but it enabled subsequent studies at the Mayo Clinic to disclose that a combination of sulfadiazine and streptomycin is useful in this disease.

The means for control of accidental infections that were developed at Camp Detrick during the war have proved valuable not only in research with highly infective agents there and elsewhere but also in work that requires the exclusion of germs, as in the commercial production of biologicals like liver extracts, which must be handled in a germ-free environment because they are damaged by any attempt to sterilize them with heat or chemicals. Many of these infections occurred under the "mysterious" conditions that had by then become characteristic of such accidents in research with highly infective agents; there was no recognizable event to explain the infection, no needle prick or puncture, no break in technique or evidence of carelessness. This sort of thing had long encouraged the suspicion of air-borne infection, but the experiences at Camp Detrick settled the matter beyond a reasonable doubt. Three kinds of proof were brought forth. One of these has not been reported on, so that I can say no more about it.* Another was the demonstration by photographic techniques, using stroboscopic light with speeds of $\frac{1}{50000}$ to $\frac{1}{100000}$ of a second, of the existence of particles in the air sprayed by routine bacteriological operations like shaking a bottle or blowing fluid out of a pipette. The third, already described in Chap. 7, was the demonstration that infection could actually take place by such means, by showing that an air-borne cloud of germs 2 feet from the point of impact of a very fine jet of fluid against the palm of the hand was sufficient to account for a case of psittacosis.

The equipment and methods used at Camp Detrick for "safety" against air-borne infections were actually devised before this proof was available but on the assumption, which these experiments validated, that air-borne transit was responsible for the laboratory infections of hitherto obscure

---

* I could not say even this much were it not for the fact that at least two references to this work have been made, without details, in the form: "Dack, G.M., 1945, Personal Communication." I should have liked to credit this work more directly, but unfortunately I have seen no published report of it.

origin. Such installations as that used for the studies of experimental air-borne infection, designed in accordance with this assumption, helped in turn to prove it; for they were used with complete safety under what would otherwise have been considered extremely hazardous conditions. Some of the same protective methods have since been applied in the new infectious-disease building of the National Institute of Health and in other laboratories where dangerous germs are studied; some have also been put to use in the more advanced pharmaceutical plants, where they serve the reverse purpose of keeping contaminating bacteria out of a system in which products that cannot be sterilized are processed and packed.

The experiments at Camp Detrick on infection carried through the air have also made available exact methods and refined techniques to attack the most important group of human diseases still uncontrolled by sanitation—the respiratory infections, like influenza and tuberculosis.

The scientists at Camp Detrick had two kinds of help that are so rare in times of peace as to make them seem characteristic of war. They had an almost unlimited budget, and they worked cooperatively in a way that puts the departmental fences of many peacetime laboratories to shame. That money is useful to science need surprise nobody, although it is one of the facts of life that are often ignored until war makes the need for science inescapable. But cooperative research was as important as money at Camp Detrick and as much a product of war. Working together or with ample facilities for cooperation were bacteriologists, physiologists, pathologists, chemists, physicians, veterinarians, botanists, physicists, engineers, machinists, and a variety of men with other skills. They did not always work in perfect harmony, since the war disclosed no magic formula to abolish personal jealousy and friction. The newly coined word "snafu" was appreciated at Camp Detrick as much as it was in any military establishment. But there was plenty of material and man power; the facilities for cooperation were at hand; and the common war effort made it possible to bring them all together and get a job done which, in retrospect, seems to me little less than magnificent.

The facilities for cooperative research—the British call it "operational research"—were built into the fabric of Camp Detrick as they have been into few other large American installations for biological work. It is coming to be recognized more and more generally that the great unconquered illnesses of man—like cancer, heart disease, and the respiratory infections—demand this very sort of installation for their conquest. But if there is anything quite like Camp Detrick beyond the rolling hills of Maryland it, too, is probably being used now for BW.

There is something else good at Camp Detrick, something closer to the heart of BW itself, which could be eminently constructive and valuable if applied to peace rather than to war. This is the idea that infective disease can be produced artificially with greater ease and freedom than is done naturally by uncontrolled forces. This idea, which BW might leave as its legacy to a peaceful world, might generate an experimental exploration of natural epidemic diseases as fruitful for human welfare as the older experimental bacteriology which, since Pasteur's day, has revolutionized our ability to deal with infection in individuals. By experimentation on animal populations with a view to the conquest, in particular, of the great air-borne epidemics, we might learn to control them as effectively as we can now control cholera and typhoid fever through water sanitation. There have been few reported attempts to tackle this subject of experimental epidemiology. The field is difficult; it requires costly apparatus, a large budget, and plenty of assistance. Camp Detrick is ready-made for the job both physically and in its technical and ideological background. It could be converted to this eminently useful purpose and to many others of like value, if only we had peace.

Camp Detrick was born of fear. It now helps to generate more fear and is thereby itself regenerated. While fear remains Camp Detrick and its sister stations throughout the world must go on storing up destruction. If we had peace, these places could show us how to abolish influenza and the common cold, tuberculosis, malaria, and all the other natural plagues of man, as well as those of animals and plants. There is no reason to doubt that these things could be done; but first we must abolish the unnatural plague of war.

SOURCES

General

HISTORICAL
A bibliography of papers on BW published from 1927 to 1941, some of which are cited below, appears on pp. 88-89 of the 1942 Report.

OFFICIAL
MERCK, GEORGE W., "Report to the Secretary of War on Biological Warfare" [the Merck Report]. *Military Surgeon, 98:* 237, March, 1946; also *Bulletin of the Atomic Scientists, 2:* 16, October 1, 1946. Condensed in *The New York Times,* January 4, 1946.

MERCK, GEORGE W., "Peacetime Implications of Biological Warfare" [the Westinghouse Forum address]. *Chemical and Engineering News, 24:* 1346, May 25, 1946.

MERCK, G. W., E. B. FRED, I. L. BALDWIN, and W. B. SARLES, "Implications of Biological Warfare." The United States and the United Nations Report Series No. 5, Scientific Information Transmitted to the UNAEC, June 14, 1946–October 14, 1946. Prepared in the Office of Mr. Bernard M. Baruch. United States Government Printing Office, Department of State Publication No. 2661, Vol. 1, Part y, p. 65.

Navy Department press release, January 4, 1946. Condensed in *The New York Times,* January 5, 1946.

UNOFFICIAL
ROSEBURY, T., E. A. KABAT, and M. H. BOLDT, "Bacterial Warfare" [the 1942 Report]. *Journal of Immunology, 56:* 7, May, 1947.

Magazine articles on BW in addition to those referred to in the text and cited below include:

ANONYMOUS, "Bacteria As Weapons of War." *Pharmaceutical Journal, 156:* 40, January 19, 1946.

SHALLET, SIDNEY, "The Deadliest War." *Collier's,* June 15, 1946.

CARTER, DYSON, "New Ways of Killing." *New Masses,* September 3, 1946.

PIEL, GERARD, "BW." *Life,* November 18, 1946.

ENGEL, LEONARD, "The Scope of Biological Warfare." *The Nation,* July 26, 1947.

FEINER, JEROME, "If Biological Warfare Comes." *Harpers,* May, 1948.

MAYER, R. L., "Epidemics and Bacteriological Warfare." *The Scientific Monthly, 67:* 331, November, 1948.

Chapter 1

"Camp Detrick Will Continue as Laboratory." *Frederick* [Maryland] *Post,* January 25, 1946.

"Camp Detrick Parent Research Center of New Type of Warfare." *Frederick News,* July 7, 1946.

BALDWIN, HANSON W., "Germ War Is Studied." *The New York Times,* September 27, 1946.

"Army Secrets Get Airing in Congress Talks" [AP story]. *New York Herald Tribune,* May 24, 1948.

Chapter 2

"U.S. Studying Atom and Germ Warfare Defenses" [AP story]. *New York Herald Tribune,* December 1, 1947.

"Army Is Silent on Germ Warfare" [AP story]. *The New York Sun,* January 23, 1947.

"Army Bans News on Germ Weapons" [UP story]. *New York Herald Tribune,* September 15, 1947.

"Conspiracy of Silence Hides Tests." *PM,* September 15, 1947.

"Hush on Germ Warfare" [editorial]. *San Francisco Chronicle,* January 27, 1947.

ANONYMOUS, "Policy at the Crossroads; an Informal Summary

SOURCES 201

Record of the Policy Developments concerning the International Control of Atomic Energy, October 15, 1946, to May 17, 1948." United States Government Printing Office, Department of State Publication No. 3161, p. 2.

Chapter 4

LeRENARD, A., "La guerre bactériologique." *La Tunisie Médicale, 30:* 413, December, 1936.

Laboratory infections were reported from Camp Detrick as follows:

ELLINGSON, H. V., P. J. KADULL, H. L. BOOKWALTER, and C. HOWE, "Cutaneous Anthrax: Report of Twenty-five Cases." *Journal of the American Medical Association, 131:* 1105, August 3, 1946.

HOWE, C., and W. R. MILLER, "Human Glanders: Report of Six Cases." *Annals of Internal Medicine, 26:* 93, January, 1947.

HOWE, C., E. S. MILLER, E. H. KELLY, H. L. BOOKWALTER, and H. V. ELLINGSON, "Acute Brucellosis among Laboratory Workers." *New England Journal of Medicine, 236:* 741, May 15, 1947.

HOWE, C., L. L. CORIELL, H. L. BOOKWALTER, and H. V. ELLINGSON, "Streptomycin Treatment in Tularemia." *Journal of the American Medical Association, 132:* 195, September 28, 1946.

ROSEBURY, T., H. V. ELLINGSON, G. MEIKLEJOHN, and F. M. SCHABEL, "A Laboratory Infection with Psittacosis Virus Treated with Penicillin and Sulfadiazine, and Experimental Data Bearing on the Mode of Infection." *Journal of Infectious Diseases, 80:* 64, January–February, 1947.

Chapter 5

"Congressmen Reveal Germ Weapon Can Wipe Out City at Single Blow" [AP story]. *The New York Times,* May 25, 1946.

"Germ Weapon Called Just a Mighty Rumor" [AP story]. *New York World-Telegram,* May 25, 1946.

"Better Than the Bomb." *Time,* June 30, 1946.

LAMANNA, C., O. E. MCELROY, and H. W. EKLUND, "The Purification and Crystallization of Clostridium botulinum Type A Toxin." *Science, 103:* 613, May 17, 1946.

ABRAMS, A., G. KEGELES, and G. A. HOTTLE, "The Purification of Toxin from Clostridium botulinum." *Journal of Biological Chemistry, 164:* 63, July, 1946.

SPECIAL PROJECTS DIVISION, CHEMICAL WARFARE SERVICE, CAMP DETRICK, MARYLAND, "Plant Growth Regulators." *Science, 103:* 469, April 19, 1946.

NORMAN, A. G., and OTHERS, "Studies on Plant Growth-regulating Substances." *Botanical Gazette, 107:* 475, June, 1946.

NORMAN, A. G., "Agronomic Uses for Plant Growth-regulators." *Journal of the American Society of Agronomy, 40:* 111, February, 1948.

ANDERSON, A. L., B. W. HENRY, and E. C. TULLIS, "Factors Affecting Infectivity, Spread, and Persistence of Piricularia oryzae Cav." *Phytopathology, 37:* 94, February, 1947.

PAGE, R. M., A. F. SHERF, and T. L. MORGAN, "The Effect of Temperature and Relative Humidity on the Longevity of the Conidia of Helminthosporium oryzae." *Mycologia, 39:* 158, March–April, 1947.

SHERF, A. F., R. M. PAGE, E. C. TULLIS, and T. L. MORGAN, "Studies on Factors Affecting the Infectivity of Helminthosporium oryzae." *Phytopathology, 37:* 281, May, 1947.

SNIESZKO, S. F., B. CARPENTER, E. P. LOWE, and J. G. JAKOB, "Improved Methods for the Cultivation and Storage of Phytophthora infestans." *Phytopathology, 37:* 635, September, 1947.

WEINSTEIN, I., "An Outbreak of Smallpox in New York City." *American Journal of Public Health, 37:* 1376, November, 1947.

WAITT, ALDEN H., "Gas Warfare. Smoke, Flame and Gas in Modern War." Washington, *The Infantry Journal,* second edition, April, 1944.

Chapter 6

FOX, L. A., "Bacterial Warfare. The Use of Biologic Agents in Warfare." *Military Surgeon, 72:* 189, March, 1933.

FRANCIS, E., "Longevity of the Tick Ornithodorus turicata and of Spirochaeta recurrentis within this Tick." *United States Public Health Reports*, 53: 2220, December 23, 1938.

Chapter 7

"Weapon against Botulism Forged through Research." *Science News Letter*, May 25, 1946.

"Ounce of New Superpoison Held Able to Wipe Out U.S., Canada." *The New York Times*, September 19, 1946.

WENDT, GERALD, "Silent Death." *Science Illustrated*, October, 1946.

"Waitt Confirms New Superpoison." *The New York Times*, September 20, 1946.

LAMANNA, C., O. E. McELROY, and H. W. EKLUND, "The Purification and Crystallization of Clostridium botulinum Type A Toxin." *Science*, 103: 613, May 17, 1946.

ABRAMS, A., G. KEGELES, and G. A. HOTTLE, "The Purification of Toxin from Clostridium botulinum." *Journal of Biological Chemistry*, 164: 63, July, 1946.

GUYTON, A. C., and M. A. MACDONALD, "Physiology of Botulinus Toxin." *Archives of Neurology and Psychiatry*, 57: 258, May, 1947.

Population data are taken from the *World Almanac* for 1948.

DOWNS, C. M., L. L. CORIELL, G. B. PINCHOT, E. MAUMENEE, A. KLAUBER, S. S. CHAPMAN, and B. OWEN, "Studies on Tularemia: I. The Comparative Susceptibility of Various Laboratory Animals." *Journal of Immunology*, 56: 217, July, 1947.

HAMBURGER, M., T. T. PUCK, V. G. HAMBURGER, and M. A. JOHNSON, "Studies on the Transmission of Hemolytic Streptococcus Infections: III. Hemolytic Streptococci in the Air, Floor Dust, and Bedclothing of Hospital Wards and their Relation to Cross Infection." *Journal of Infectious Diseases*, 75: 79, July–August, 1944.

ROSEBURY, T., H. V. ELLINGSON, G. MEIKLEJOHN, and F. M. SCHABEL, "A Laboratory Infection with Psittacosis Virus Treated with Penicillin and Sulfadiazine, and Experimental Data Bearing on the Mode of Infection." *Journal of Infectious Diseases*, 80: 64, January–February, 1947.

Chapter 8

Lewis, K. H., and E. V. Hill, "Practical Media and Control Measures for Producing Highly Toxic Cultures of Clostridium botulinum, Type A." *Journal of Bacteriology*, 53: 213, February, 1947.

Miller, W. R., L. Pannell, L. Cravitz, W. A. Tanner, and M. S. Ingalls, "Studies on Certain Biological Characteristics of Malleomyces mallei and Malleomyces pseudomallei: I. Morphology, Cultivation, Viability, and Isolation from Contaminated Specimens." *Journal of Bacteriology*, 55: 115, January, 1948.

Gerhardt, P., "Brucella suis in Aerated Broth Culture: III. Continuous Culture Studies." *Journal of Bacteriology*, 52: 283, September, 1946.

Kaplan, A. M., and S. Elberg, "Concentration of Brucella suis from Broth Culture." *Journal of Bacteriology*, 52: 513, November, 1946.

Glassman, H. N., and S. Elberg, "The Growth of Brucella in Aerated Liquid Cultures." *Journal of Bacteriology*, 52: 523, October, 1946.

Roessler, W. G., E. J. Herbst, W. G. McCullough, R. C. Mills, and C. R. Brewer, "Studies with Coccidioides immitis: I. Submerged Growth in Liquid Mediums." *Journal of Infectious Diseases*, 79: 12, July–August, 1946.

Rosebury, T., M. H. Boldt, F. R. Olson, J. Aaron, N. G. Cournoyer, D. R. Cameron, A. Rosenwald, C. Franzen, C. E. O'Bryon, E. P. Neff, H. Kress, and D. M. Kehn, *Experimental Air-borne Infection*. The Williams & Wilkins Company, Baltimore, 1947.

Chapter 9

Rochaix, A., "Epidémies provoqués à propos de la guerre bactérienne." *Revue d'Hygiene*, 58: 161, March, 1936.

LeRenard, A., "La guerre bactériologique." *La Tunisie Médicale*, 30: 413, December, 1936.

de Flers, Robert, *Sur les chemins de la guerre*. Lafitte, Paris, 1919, p. 129.

LeBourdelles: "La guerre bactériologique et la défense passive antimicrobienne." *Le Bulletin médicale* [Paris], 53[1]: 179, March 11, 1939.

Duffour, J., "La guerre bactériologique." *Journal de Médicin de Bordeaux, 114:* 333, October 16, 1937.

"Aggressive war against the U.S.S.R." [Section of the summary of the verdict of the International Military Tribunal at Nuremberg, September 30, 1946]. *The New York Times,* October 1, 1946.

Steed, Wickham, "Aerial warfare: secret German plans." *The Nineteenth Century and After* [London], 689: 1, July, 1934.

Waksman, Selman A., "Science—salvation or destroyer of mankind?" *Bulletin of America's Town Meeting of the Air, 12:* 3, May 16, 1946.

"Bacteriological warfare" [editorial]. *Medical Record, 155:* 269, April 15, 1942.

Newman, Barclay M., *Japan's Secret Weapon.* Current Publishing Company, New York, 1944, p. 20.

Rand, Christopher, "Bubonic Plague Spreads North to Hitherto-free Central China." *New York Herald Tribune,* January 28, 1948.

Rosebury, T., M. H. Boldt, F. R. Olson, J. Aaron, N. G. Cournoyer, D. R. Cameron, A. Rosenwald, C. Franzen, C. E. O'Bryon, E. P. Neff, H. Kress, and D. M. Kehn, *Experimental Air-borne Infection.* The Williams & Wilkins Company, Baltimore, 1947.

Chapter 10

Winchell, Walter [column], *New York Daily Mirror,* October 14, 1947.

"Egypt Alleges Germ Warfare" [UP story]. *PM,* May 28, 1948.

Biraud, T., and P. M. Kaul, "World Distribution and Prevalence of Cholera in Recent Years." *Epidemiological and Vital Statistics Report,* W.H.O. Interim Commission, *1:* 140, December, 1947.

United States Navy Coveralls for Use in Germ and Poison Warfare [photographs]. *Newsweek,* January 14, 1946, p. 76; also *Science News Letter,* January 12, 1946, p. 21.

REYNIERS, J. A., "Germ-free Life Studies." Lobund Reports, University of Notre Dame, No. 1, November, 1946.

Chapter 11

"The Report of President Truman on the Atomic Bomb, August 6, 1945." *Science, 102:* 163, August 17, 1945.

STIMSON, HENRY L., "The Decision to Use the Atomic Bomb." *Harpers,* February, 1947.

ANONYMOUS, "A Report to the Secretary of War, June, 1945." *Bulletin of the Atomic Scientists, 1:* 2, May 1, 1946.

"Einstein Deplores Use of Atom Bomb." *The New York Times,* August 19, 1946.

"Atomic Energy and American Policy: Official and Unofficial Pronouncements" [statement by Secretary of War Stimson, August 6, 1945]. International Conciliation, Carnegie Endowment for International Peace, No. 416, December, 1945, p. 764.

President Truman's foreign-policy address, October 27, 1945. International Conciliation, Carnegie Endowment for International Peace, No. 416, December, 1945, p. 779.

Foreign Minister Molotov's speech, November 6, 1945. International Conciliation, Carnegie Endowment for International Peace, No. 416, December, 1945, p. 757.

"Truman-Attlee-King Declaration on Atomic Energy, November 15, 1945." International Conciliation, Carnegie Endowment for International Peace, No. 416, December, 1945, p. 787; also *The New York Times,* November 16, 1945.

Text of the Moscow Conference of December 16 to 26, 1945. *PM,* December 28, 1946.

"The Control of Atomic Energy: Proposals before the UNAEC and Unofficial Plans" [UN General Assembly resolution on atomic energy of January 24, 1946]. International Conciliation, Carnegie Endowment for International Peace, No. 423, September, 1946, p. 333; also *The New York Times,* January 26, 1946.

"A Report on the International Control of Atomic Energy" [the Acheson-Lilienthal Report]. Prepared for the Secretary of State's Committee on Atomic Energy by a Board of Consultants. United

States Government Printing Office, Department of State Publication No. 2498, March 16, 1946.

Bernard M. Baruch's address before the UN Atomic Energy Commission, June 14, 1946. *The New York Times,* June 15, 1946.

"Poland to Ask UN to Ban Bacteriological Warfare" [UP story]. *PM,* October 3, 1947.

Andrei A. Gromyko's address before the UN Atomic Energy Commission, June 19, 1946. *The New York Times,* June 20, 1946.

Mr. Gromyko's speech to the American-Russian Institute, May 19, 1947. *The New York Times,* May 20, 1947.

Foreign Minister Molotov's speech before the UN General Assembly, October 29, 1946. *The New York Times,* October 30, 1946.

SHILS, EDWARD A., "The Failure of the UNAEC: An Interpretation." *Bulletin of the Atomic Scientists,* 4: 205, July, 1948.

ANONYMOUS, "Policy at the Crossroads; an Informal Summary Record of the Policy Developments concerning the International Control of Atomic Energy, October 15, 1946, to May 17, 1948." United States Government Printing Office, Department of State Publication No. 3161, p. 2.

LeRENARD, A., "La guerre bactériologique." *La Tunisie Médicale, 30:* 413, December, 1936.

DAVIES, JOSEPH E., *Mission to Moscow.* Simon and Schuster, Inc., New York, 1941, p. 278.

HINDUS, MAURICE, "Land Reform Only Hope of Middle East" [article on Russian BW]. *Montreal Herald,* January 27, 1948.

"Warns of Bacteria War" [AP story]. *New York Herald Tribune,* March 29, 1948.

Mr. Gromyko's speech before the UN Security Council, February 14, 1947. *The New York Times,* February 15, 1947.

"Soviet Paper Says Japan Planned Germ Warfare" [AP story]. *New York Herald Tribune,* July 29, 1948.

Chapter 12

"Marshall Sets All Battle Dead at 15,000,000." *New York Herald Tribune,* November 3, 1947.

Other data on casualties and dollar costs of World War II are from the *World Almanac* for 1948.

ANONYMOUS, "Economic Consequences of a Third World War." *Business Week*, April 24, 1948.

Chapter 13

OTTEN, L., "Immunization against Plague with Live Vaccine." *Indian Journal of Medical Research, 24:* 73, July, 1936.

WAGLE, P. M., S. S. SOKHEY, S. B. DIKSHIT, and K. GANAPATHY, "Chemotherapy in Plague." *Indian Medical Gazette, 76:* 29, January, 1941.

James G. Byrnes' speech at Charleston, South Carolina, November 16, 1945. *The New York Times*, November 17, 1945.

LIPPMANN, WALTER, *One World or None*. Whittlesey House (McGraw-Hill Book Company, Inc.), New York, 1946, Chap. 13.

ROMIEU: "La guerre microbienne." *Revue des Deux Mondes*, September 1, 1934, p. 41.

LAURENCE, WILLIAM L., "Scientists Assail Bacteria Warfare." *The New York Times*, July 27, 1947.

Chapter 14

NORMAN, A. G., and OTHERS, "Studies on Plant Growth-regulating Substances." *Botanical Gazette, 107:* 475, June, 1946.

KEGELES, G., "The Molecular Size and Shape of Botulinus Toxin." *Journal of the American Chemical Society, 68:* 1670, 1946.

PUTNAM, F. W., C. LAMANNA, and D. G. SHARP, "Molecular Weight and Homogeneity of Crystalline Botulinus A Toxin." *Journal of Biological Chemistry, 165:* 735, October, 1946.

BUEHLER, H. J., E. J. SCHANTZ, and C. LAMANNA, "The Elemental and Amino Acid Composition of Crystalline Botulinus Type A Toxin." *Journal of Biological Chemistry, 169:* 295, July, 1947.

LAMANNA, C., and H. N. GLASSMAN, "The Isolation of Type B Botulinum Toxin." *Journal of Bacteriology, 54:* 575, November, 1947.

BRANDLEY, C. A., H. E. MOSES, E. L. JUNGHERR, E. E. JONES, and

E. E. TYZZER, "Newcastle Disease and Fowl Plague Investigations in the War Research Program." *Journal of the American Veterinary Medical Association, 108:* 369, June, 1946.

BRANDLEY, C. A., and OTHERS, Papers on Newcastle Disease. *American Journal of Veterinary Research, 7:* 243, July, 1946.

SHOPE, R. E., and OTHERS, Papers on Rinderpest Virus. *American Journal of Veterinary Research, 7:* 133, April, 1946.

HOTTLE, G. A., and A. ABRAMS, "Detoxification of Crystalline Botulinum Type A Toxin." *Journal of Immunology, 55:* 183, February, 1947.

HOTTLE, G. A., C. NIGG, and J. A. LICHTY, "Studies on Botulinum Toxoid, Types A and B: II. Methods for Determining Antigenicity in Animals." *Journal of Immunology, 55:* 255, March, 1947.

NIGG, C., G. A. HOTTLE, L. L. CORIELL, A. S. ROSENWALD, and G. W. BEVERIDGE, "Studies on Botulinus Toxoids, Types A and B: I. Production of Alum Precipitated Toxoids." *Journal of Immunology, 55:* 245, March, 1947.

REAMES, H. R., and P. J. KADULL, "Studies on Botulinus Toxoids, Types A and B: Immunization of Man." *Journal of Immunology, 55:* 209, April, 1947.

WAGNER, J. C., G. MEIKLEJOHN, L. C. KINGSLAND, and H. W. HICKISH, "Psittacosis Vaccines Prepared from Chick Embryo Tissues." *Journal of Immunology, 54:* 85, September, 1946.

CROMARTIE, W. J., D. W. WATSON, W. L. BLOOM, R. J. HECKLY, G. KEGELES, M. FREED, W. J. McGHEE, and N. WEISSMAN, "Studies on Infection with Bacillus anthracis." *Journal of Infectious Diseases, 80:* 1, January–February; 121, March–April, 1947.

MILLER, W. R., L. PANNELL, and M. S. INGALLS, "Experimental Chemotherapy in Glanders and Melioidosis." *American Journal of Hygiene, 47:* 205, March, 1948.

MILLER, E. S., E. B. SCOTT, H. A. NOE, S. H. MADIN, and T. F. HENLEY, "Chemotherapy of Experimental Anthrax Infection." *Journal of Immunology, 53:* 271, August, 1946.

SCHABEL, F. M., H. R. REAMES, and R. D. HOUSEWRIGHT, "The Use of Sulfadiazine and Penicillin for Treatment of Experimental Anthrax." *Journal of Infectious Diseases, 79:* 141, September–October, 1946.

HOUSEWRIGHT, R. D., S. BERKMAN, and R. J. HENRY, "The Relative Effectiveness of Pure Penicillins against Bacillus anthracis in Vitro and in Vivo." *Journal of Immunology, 57:* 343, December, 1947.

MEIKLEJOHN, G., J. C. WAGNER, G. W. BEVERIDGE, R. W. WISEMAN, and D. B LACKMAN, "Studies on the Chemotherapy of Viruses in the Psittacosis-lymphogranuloma Group." *Journal of Immunology, 54:* 1, September, 1946.

EARLY, R. L., and H. R. MORGAN, "Studies on the Chemotherapy of Viruses in the Psittacosis-lymphogranuloma Venereum Group." *Journal of Immunology, 53:* 151, June; 251, July, 1946.

JOHANSSON, K. R., and D. H. FERRIS, "Photography of Airborne Particles during Bacteriological Plating Operations." *Journal of Infectious Diseases, 78:* 238, May–June, 1946.

For papers on laboratory infections, which include treatment of infections in man, see sources for Chap. 4.

ROSEBURY, T., M. H. BOLDT, F. R. OLSON, J. AARON, N. G. COURNOYER, D. R. CAMERON, A. ROSENWALD, C. FRANZEN, C. E. O'BRYON, E. P. NEFF, H. KRESS, and D. M. KEHN, *Experimental Air-borne Infection.* The Williams & Wilkins Company, Baltimore, 1947.

INDEX

A

ABC Committee, 7
Abrams, Adolph, 78, 187
Acheson-Lilienthal Report, 140, 143
Actinomycetes, 20
Agents of infection, 19, 29
  of animals, 53
  of animals and man, 54
  of animals and plants, 51
  clouds of, 114
  of man, 52
  modification of, 45, 133
  of plants, 55
  selection of, for BW, 62
Air-borne BW, alleged German, 107
  particle size in, 113
Air-borne infection, 27, 112
  artificial, 45
  defense against, 121
  peacetime implications of, 195
Air-borne laboratory infections, 46, 83, 96, 194
Air incineration, 96
Air sanitation, 129
Amherst, 108
Animal experiments, 36, 172
Animal pests, destruction of, 105
Animals, BW in, 111
  defense against, 135
Anthrax, 49, 54, 56, 191
  bacillus, 74, 82, 191
  and German BW, 106
  spores, dissemination of, 113
    stability of, 71
  treatment of, 193
  vaccine for, 132, 135, 190, 191
Antibodies, 32
Antitoxins, 32
Athlete's foot, 27
Atomic bomb, and BW compared, 149, 151, 176
  decision to use, 138
  history of, 137
Atomic energy, and BW, peacetime value compared, 186
  control of, 139
  practicability of, 148
Atomization, 113
Austin, Warren R., 141

B

Bacilli, 22
Backfiring of BW, 44, 74, 101, 102
Bacteria, 20, 22

Bacteria, cultures of, 69
  production of, 89
Baldwin, Hanson W., 9
Bang's Disease (*see* Brucellosis)
Baruch, Bernard, 140, 141
Baruch Plan, 140, 144
Bayard, 178
BW agents, availability of, 88
  casualty effectiveness of, 67
  combination of, 45
  criterion for selection of, 62, 68
  detection of, 74, 122
  epidemicity of, 72
  identification of, 123
  infectivity of, 63
  immunization against, 73
  means of transmission of, 72
  production materials for, 90
  resistance of, 71
  retroactivity of, 74
  selection of, 62
  stability of, 71, 95, 115
  therapy against, 73
  transmission of, 72
Black, Henry M., 9
Black Death, 44
Blast disease of cattle, 55
Boldt, Martin H., 6
Botulinus toxins, 41, 54, 58, 75, 77–81, 100
  crystalline, 77, 187
  dosage of, 77
  production of, 92
Botulinus toxoids, 131, 132, 190
Botulism, 41, 54, 78
Bouquet, 108
Breakbone fever, 43, 53, 73
British BW, 7, 8, 13
Brown-spot disease of rice, 55
Brucella, detection of, 74
  production of, 93

Brucellosis, 42, 49, 56, 58, 82, 111
  air-borne, 46, 115
  in animals and man, 28, 54
  treatment of, 42, 193
  vaccine for, 132
Burkhardt, Ernst, 107
Byrnes, James F., 140, 175

C

Camp Detrick, appropriation for, 9, 10
  BW production at, 92
  laboratory infections at, 49, 84, 96, 193
  peacetime uses of, 185
  plan for, 7
  postwar program at, 9
  sewage sterilization at, 97
  studies at, of air-borne infection, 114, 194
    of BW production, 92
    of botulinus toxins, 54, 77, 187
    of plant-growth regulators, 55, 187
    of plant infections, 55
    of vaccines, 189
  technical reports from, 15, 92, 186
Canadian BW, 7, 8, 13, 189
Capsule, 22, 23, 32, 192
Casualties in World War II, 161
Casualty effectiveness, 67
Cerebrospinal meningitis, 37, 39, 52, 72, 119
Chemical agents, dissemination of, 103
Chemical Warfare Service, 7, 9, 61

Chicken pox, 70, 119
Cholera, 37, 52, 111, 118, 120, 196
   and alleged German BW, 107
   in Egypt, 125
   vibrio, 26, 39
Civilian defense, 128
Clothing, protective, 130
"Clouds" of infective agents, 114–116
Cocci, 22
Coccidioides immitis, 71, 93
Coccidioidomycosis, 53, 93
Common cold, 119, 197
Communicable, definition of, 29
Congress of Microbiology resolution, 178
Contact, infection by, 27
Contagious, definition of, 29
Conventions, international, 178, 180
Cooperative research, 196
Cost, of BW agents, 89
   of BW development, 91
   of BW production, 90
   of peace, 160
   of preventing war, 164, 167
   of war, 161, 167
Cowpox, 24, 33
Criteria for selection of BW agents, 62–76
Cultures, 69
   for production of BW agents, 89
Cytological Congress resolution, 179

D

2,4-dichlorophenoxyacetic acid (2,4-D), 55, 103, 111, 186

Davies, Joseph E., 150
DEF Committee, 7
Dengue, 43, 53, 70, 73
Detection, 122
   criterion for BW agents, 74
Diabetes, 36
Diphtheria, 32, 131
   toxin, 78
Dissemination, air-borne, 112
   of BW agents, 86
   of 2,4-D, 103
   devices for, 94
   problem of, 103
Dosage-infection curve, 65
Drugs in defense, 133
   studies of, at Camp Detrick, 193
Duffour, J., 113
Dysentery, alleged BW in Egypt, 125
   bacillary, 52

E

Economic effects of BW, 60
Effectiveness of BW, 99
Effects of BW, 58
   on animals and plants, 60
Einstein, Albert, 138
Encephalitis, 54, 131
Epidemicity, as criterion of BW agents, 72
   and retroactivity, 75
Epidemics, 28
   artificial, 39
   control of, 118
   experimental, 40, 196
Epidemiology, 35, 40
Equine encephalomyelitis, 54
Equipment, for BW development, 96

Equipment, for BW production, 92
Ethics and war, 174

F

Field testing, 7, 99
Fog generator, 103
Foot-and-mouth disease, 53, 111
Forman, Harrison, 109
Fowl cholera, 105
Fowl plague, 54, 189
Francis, Edward, 72
Fungi, 20, 27, 53, 71, 93, 111

G

Gas warfare, 61
Geneva Protocol, 179
German BW, 8, 13, 106, 150
German measles, 70
Glanders, 49, 54
  air-borne, 46, 115
  bacillus, production of, 93
  and German BW, 106
  treatment of, 193
  vaccine for, 132
Gonococcus, 27
Gonorrhea, 28, 37, 118
Gromyko, Andrei A., 140, 144, 150, 178
Grosse Ile, 189
Groves, Leslie R., 139
Growth regulators for plants, 55, 187

H

Hague Convention, 179
Hemorrhagic septicemia, 53
d'Herelle, F., 106

Hindus, Maurice, 150
History of BW, 105
History of U.S. BW program, 5
Hog cholera, 54
Human experimentation, 66, 171, 172, 190

I

Ideal weapon, 61
Identification of BW agents, 123
Immunity, definition of, 32
Immunization, as criterion for BW agents, 73
  in defense, 131
Immunology, 34
Incapacitation versus killing, 58, 135
Incubation period, 30, 56, 86
Infection, 24
  air-borne, 27, 45, 112, 121, 195
  control of, 119
  and dosage, 65
  entrance of, 26
  experimental, 36
  prevention of, 118
  recovery from, 30
  specificity of, 25
  transmission of, 27
  (See also Laboratory infections)
Infective, definition of, 29
Infectivity, 30, 48
  of clouds, 114–116
  as criterion for BW agents, 63
  for man, 66, 82
  measurement of, 66
  and retroactivity, 75
Inflammation, 31
Influenza, 24, 53, 119, 131, 197
Insects, destruction of, 106

INDEX

International control, of atomic energy, 139
of BW, 149
Isolation in defense, 127

J

Japanese BW, 8, 13, 109, 150
Jenner, Edward, 33
Johnson, Edwin C., 150

K

Kabat, Elvin A., 6

L

Laboratory infections, 46, 83, 96
at Camp Detrick, 49, 192
prevention of, 95
Lamanna, Carl, 77, 92, 187, 188
Late blight of potatoes, 55
Lateran, Council of, 178
LD_{50}, 65, 85
Leprosy, 68, 70
Le Renard, A., 43, 150
Lewis, Sinclair, 173
Lie, Trygvie, 142
Lightning war, 159
Lilienthal, David E., 139
Limits of BW, 51, 56
Lippmann, Walter, 175
Loir, Dr., 105
Lymphogranuloma venereum, 28

M

Malaria, 28, 53, 73, 118, 120, 197
protozoan, 26, 28
Man, value of, 170
Marshall, George C., 161
Masks in defense, 130

Measles, 53, 119
Melioidosis, 52, 58, 132
air-borne, 65, 115
bacillus, production of, 93
infection-dosage curve for, 65
Merck, George W., 5, 6, 7, 8, 9, 13, 14, 97, 109
Merck Report, 7, 8, 9, 13, 14, 16, 49, 99, 106, 109, 123
Metchnikoff, Elie, 106
Micron, 22
Molotov, Vyacheslav M., 139, 145
Moral judgments of BW, 175, 181
Mouse typhoid, 106
Mumps, 53, 70, 119
Munitions, 94

N

Nazis, human experiments of, 66, 171
Newcastle disease, 54, 189
Nicolle, Charles, 108
Nucleus, 23

O

Objectives of BW, 52, 102

P

Parasitism, 25
selectivity of, 51, 56
Parran, Thomas, 109
Pasteur, Louis, 34, 105, 190, 196
Peacetime value of BW, 196
Personnel for BW, 92
Physician, ethics and, 181
Plague, 52, 58, 75, 83, 118
and alleged BW in China, 109

Plague, bubonic, 37, 120
  human experiments on, 172
  infectivity of, 67
  pneumonic, 44, 57, 100
  vaccine for, 132
Plant growth regulators, 55, 187
Plants, BW in, 111
  defense against, 135
Pleuropneumonia, 53
  organisms, 20
Pneumococcus, 26, 32, 37
  infectivity of, for mice, 81
Pneumonia, 26, 37, 119, 132
Poliomyelitis, 39, 53
Preventive war, 158
Production plant for BW, 8
Protozoa, 20
Psittacosis, 46, 49, 53, 58, 86
  treatment of, 193
  vaccine for, 132, 190
  virus, clouds of, 115
    dosage of, for man, 84
Psychological effects of BW, 58, 67
Public health, problems of, 120
Publication, official policy on, 16
Pus, 31
Pyorrhea, 67

Q

Quarantine in defense, 127

R

Rabies, 26, 57, 68, 131
Rats, destruction of, 106
Reed, Walter, 46
Relapsing fever, 52, 70, 72, 73
1942 Report, 6, 15, 62, 110, 112, 120

Resistance, as criterion for BW agents, 71
  to infection, infectivity and, 63
Retaliation as defense, 135
Retroactivity, 44, 101, 102
  as criterion for BW agents, 74
Reyniers, James A., 130
Rickettsiae, 20, 46, 69, 90
Rift Valley fever, 54
Rinderpest, 53, 56, 111, 189
Ringworm, 67
Rocky Mountain spotted fever, 53, 132
Roosevelt, Franklin D., 7, 138
Rumors and BW, 125
Russian BW, 13, 125, 150

S

Sabotage, 100, 101, 104, 110
Safety, 95, 96, 195
San Joaquin Valley fever, 53, 93
Sanitation, 73, 111, 120, 128
Science and politics, 156
Scientist, 155
  in war, 174
Scrub typhus, 53
Secrecy, 9, 11, 12, 69, 128
Selection of agents for BW, 62
Shelters, 130
Shils, Edward A., 146
Shope, Richard, 189
Smallpox, 24, 33
  early use of, in BW, 108
  in New York, 59
  vaccination against, 73, 131
Smith, Theobald, 26
Smyth Report, 4, 11, 19, 139
Snake venoms, 78
Special Projects Division, 8
Spirilla, 22

Spirochetes, 20, 52, 70, 95
Spore, 22, 23
Stability of BW agents, 71, 95, 115
Stanley, Wendell M., 19
Staphylococcus, 22, 30
Steed, Wickham, 107
Stimson, Henry L., 6, 138, 139
Streptococcus, 22, 24, 26
  dosage of, for man, 83
Substitute materials for BW production, 91
Syphilis, 28, 67, 118
  spirochete, 27, 71, 119

T

Tetanus, 32
  toxin, 78, 188
  toxoid, 131
Therapy, as criterion for BW agents, 73
Toxins, 32, 78
  (*See also* Botulinus toxin)
Toxoids, 33, 131, 132, 190
Transmissible, definition of, 29
Transmission, means of, as criterion for BW agents, 72
Treatment in defense, 133
  studies of, at Camp Detrick, 193
Tree of life, 21
Truman, Harry S., 137, 139, 179
Tubercle bacillus, 26
Tuberculosis, 119, 132, 197
Tularemia, 42, 46, 49, 52, 56, 58
  air-borne, 115, 116
  bacillus, infectivity for mice, 81
    stability of, 71, 72
  treatment of, 190

Tularemia, vaccine for, 132
Typhoid bacillus, 26, 27, 33
Typhoid fever, 34, 37, 52, 111, 118, 119, 196
  and alleged BW in Egypt, 125
  vaccine for, 132
Typhus fever, 46, 53, 95, 119, 131, 132
  air-borne, 73
  rickettsia, 28

U

Undulant fever (*see* Brucellosis)
United Nations Atomic Energy Commission, autopsy reports on, 146
  and BW, 142
  failure of, 141, 153
  history of, 139, 140
  terms of reference of, 140
  U.S. State Department Report on, 147
United States Army release on BW (*see* Merck Report)
United States Biological Warfare Committee, 7
United States Department of State, Report on atomic energy by, 12, 142
  (*See also* Acheson-Lilienthal Report)
  Report on BW by, 14, 133
  Report on United Nations Atomic Energy Commission by, 147
United States Navy, cooperation of, in BW, 7
  release on BW by, 14, 130

United States Public Health Service, cooperation of, in BW, 7
United States War Department, release on BW (*see* Merck Report)

V

Vaccination, 33, 73
  in defense, 131
  human experiments on, 172
  in offense, 101
Vaccines at Camp Detrick, 189
Vaccinia, 24, 33
Variability, 57, 64
Vatican casualty data, 161
Vectors, 28
Venereal disease, 28, 37, 67, 118
Vibrio, 22
Virulence, 30, 133
Virus, 19, 20
Viruses, cultures of, 69
  production of, 90
  recognition of, 24
Vishinsky, Andrei Y., 141

W

Waitt, Alden H., 61, 77
Waksman, Selman A., 108, 110
War Research Service, 7
Washington Disarmament Conference, 179
WBC Committee, 6
Weil's disease, 53
Weinstein, Israel, 59
Wendt, Gerald, 77
Westinghouse Forum Report, 14, 97
Whooping cough, 132
Winchell, Walter, 125

Y

Yellow fever, 46, 53, 59, 95, 118, 132
  air-borne, 47, 73
  vaccine for, 90, 131
  virus, 28

Z

Zlotowski, Ignazy, 142

UNIVERSITY COLLEGE
COLLEGE LIBRARY
Date Due

AUG 2 '58			
APR 2 APR 1959	1959		
OCT 2 8 '60 ML			
	OCT 2 4 '60		
NOV 1 7 '60 ML	ML 7 '60		
NOV 9 '62 ML			
NOV 3 '63 ML			
N 12 '63 ML	12 '63		
N 23 '63 ML			
MAR 7 '64 ML			

Peace or pestilence; sci
623.456R798p C.3

3 1262 03205 6441

623.456
R798p
C.3

Printed in the USA
CPSIA information can be obtained
at www.ICGtesting.com
LVHW022153080923
757420LV00005B/401